RESEARCH DISCUSSION SERIES №8

Women in Post-Compulsory Education and Training in Wales

David Istance & Teresa Rees

Equal Opportunities Commission 1994
First Published 1994

ISBN 1 870358 28 7

EOC RESEARCH DISCUSSION SERIES

The EOC Research Discussion Series provides a
channel for the dissemination of reviews of
research and the secondary analysis of data carried
out by Research Unit staff or externally
commissioned research workers.

The views expressed in this report are those of the
authors and do not necessarily represent the views of
the Commission. The Commission is publishing
the report as a contribution to discussion and
debate.

Research Unit
Equal Opportunities Commission
Overseas House
Quay Street
Manchester M3 3HN

Also in London, Cardiff and Glasgow

CONTENTS

TABLES **Page**

ABBREVIATIONS

CDL	Career Development Loan
CEEP	European Centre of Enterprises with Public Participation
DOVE	Dulais Opportunity for Voluntary Support
EC	European Commission
EOC	Equal Opportunities Commission
ESF	European Social Fund
ET	Employment Training
ETUC	European Trade Union Confederation
EU	European Union
FE	Further education
FEFCW	Further Education Funding Council for Wales
FT	Foundation Targets
GCSE	General Certificate in Secondary Education
HE	Higher education
HEFCW	Higher Education Funding Council for Wales
ITD	Industry and Training Department
LEA	Local Education Authority
LECs	Local Enterprise Companies
NACETT	National Advisory Council for Education and Training Targets
NC	National Curriculum
NIACE	National Institute of Adult and Continuing Education
NOW	New Opportunities for Women
NTETs	National Targets for Education and Training
NVQ	National Vocational Qualification
OU	Open University
PGCE	Postgraduate Certificate of Education
TEC	Training and Enterprise Council
TEED	Training, Education and Enterprise Department
UETP	University Enterprise Training Partnership
UNICE	Union of Industrial and Employers' Confederations of Europe
VET	Vocational Education and Training
WDA	Welsh Development Agency
WETIWG	Welsh Education and Training Information Working Group
YT	Youth Training

PREFACE AND ACKNOWLEDGEMENTS

This study was commissioned by the Equal Opportunities Commission to investigate the position of women in post-compulsory education and training in Wales. We welcomed the opportunity to work on this project, bringing together statistics and research findings to map the current picture. It is clear that women's potential remains underutilised because of the barriers to their participation in education and training, and because of difficulties in translating the skills and qualifications that women have developed into recognised marketable assets in the workplace.

This small-scale project has necessarily relied considerably on existing material which a large number of individuals and organisations have made available to us at quite short notice. The organisations concerned are listed in Appendix I. We are most grateful to them for their co-operation. The interpretation of the data supplied remains our own and does not necessarily represent the views of those organisations.

We should like to thank staff of the Equal Opportunities Commission, especially Val Feld from EOC Wales, and Sue Arthur, Dave Perfect and Ed Puttick from the Manchester Office, for their guidance and assistance, and members of the Steering and Advisory Group for their good advice and support. And we should like to thank Jenny Capstick of SAUS for all her painstaking work on tables and text, and Mary Robinson of Photoscript for copy-editing the report.

David Istance
Senior Research Officer
Department of Adult Continuing Education
University of Wales
Swansea

Teresa Rees
Reader
School for Advanced Urban Studies
University of Bristol

EXECUTIVE SUMMARY

INTRODUCTION

This research report examines the position of women in post-compulsory education and training in Wales: education and training after the minimum school leaving age of 16. The study is part of the Equal Opportunities Commission's contribution to the work of Chwarae Teg in Wales.

The objectives of the study are:

- to identify key aspects of the policy context and the position of women in the labour market;

- to provide a statistical review of the position of women in education and training, giving particular attention to the quality and quantity of statistics that allow gender monitoring and identifying gaps in the statistical base;

- to analyse special initiatives for women in education and training.

Policy implications of the findings are also drawn out.

The study was limited in time and resources so secondary sources served for the review of policy, context and special initiatives, together with semi-structured interviews with key actors. The statistical mapping of the position of women in education and training drew upon both official statistics, and a survey of information compiled by other agencies including further education (FE) colleges and TECs in Wales. Published statistics are often not presented in such a way as to make the gender dimension clear; for this, considerable secondary analysis is required. The survey revealed that there were no systematic patterns of record-keeping among FE colleges and TECs. The ability to respond to requests for information on women's participation patterns therefore varied widely.

The study also drew upon the expertise of members of the project steering committee and Chwarae Teg Training and Enterprise Network Working Group.

THE POLICY CONTEXT

The field of education and training has seen major policy changes in the last five years. Some of these are the result of British Government policy, others are particular to Wales. Welsh Office now has overall responsibility for Further Education (FE), Higher Education (HE) and training, and recently launched a consultative document on developing skills, *People and Prosperity: a Challenge to Wales*. Seven TECs have been set up in Wales. Funding has been transferred to Welsh Higher and Further Education Funding Councils respectively. The removal of the trans-binary divide has meant that in addition to the six colleges of University of Wales, there is the new University of Glamorgan. With the ending of local authority control of FE there have been some college mergers. New qualifications such as the National Vocational Qualifications (NVQs) and General National Vocational Qualifications (GNVQ), and targets for education and training - the National Targets for Education and Training (NTETs) - have been established.

There are two main trends running through all these changes that pull in distinct directions. On the one hand, there is the development of **consortia and partnerships** in Wales. Chwarae Teg has acted as a catalyst for projects being developed to meet women's training needs. Welsh Office has brought together the TECs and other organisations and is developing a database on training. The Welsh TECs jointly fund their own coordinator. Wales has developed networks with the four Motor Regions of Europe, and education and training projects are an important part of those links.

At the same time, there is a trend towards the **marketisation** of education and training: market forces, shaped by formula funding, are leading to changes in the priorities and activities of colleges. While the net effect of marketisation on women's education and training is difficult to predict overall, there are risks. The new formula funding, for instance, may mean that some adult education courses which have served women well may be unprofitable. Outreach work, and provision for those women from ethnic minorities with language needs, are not as lucrative as other courses. Such effects should be closely monitored.

A major source of funding for training in Wales is the **European Commission** (EC). The EC is increasingly concerned about the need to develop women's skills. This is for both economic reasons (given demographic changes and skill shortages in the European Union) and social reasons (the need to avoid large scale social exclusion of women). There are moves to ensure that women's needs are in future mainstreamed in the European Social Fund (ESF). NOW, the EC initiative specifically to promote women's training, is set to begin a new, six-year phase with double the budget of the previous phase. IRIS, the network of women's training projects in Europe, has just begun a second, expanded phase.

Equal opportunities generally and women's needs in particular must be kept centre stage in the development of new policies.

WOMEN AND THE LABOUR MARKET IN WALES

Economic activity rates for women and men in Wales are among the lowest in Britain. A major cause of inactivity is the high number of working age men and women registered as sick and disabled. Childcare facilities are especially inadequate in Wales and are a barrier to women's participation in education, training and the labour market. The workforce is highly segregated, with many women in part-time and low skilled, low paid jobs. Some 20 percent of the population are Welsh speakers, and female Welsh speakers are more likely to be economically inactive or in low skilled jobs than non-Welsh speakers. Women from ethnic minorities constitute just over one percent of women of working age in Wales, of whom just under half are economically active compared with nearly two thirds of white women. There are variations between ethnic groups: Black African and Caribbean, Indian and Chinese women are more likely to be economically active, Pakistanis and Bangladeshis less so.

Key barriers to unemployed and economically inactive women's participation in education, training and employment have been identified as: lack of affordable childcare facilities, lack of access to private transport and inadequate public transport, lack of confidence, inappropriate hours, and lack of up-to-date substantive skills. For women wanting to return to education and training, family-friendly hours and styles of teaching, women tutors, and women-only training especially in new technologies, have also proved to be important.

Other key features of women's participation in the labour market in terms of their access to training are:

- Investment in training by employers is highly skewed towards full-time senior, managerial and technical staff; as a consequence, far too many women miss out on job related training. In sectors which are major employers of women, there are divergent trends.

- Women predominate in education and health, both of which are characterised by relatively greater investment in staff training. However, there is a danger that increased "credentialism" of the professions, implying even greater demands for qualifications, poses particular problems for women who take career breaks, or who want to return to

vii

work part-time. The skills and qualifications gap between them and men and women who have full-time continuous service will widen.

- There are relatively few women in top jobs in Wales compared with England, even in female-dominated professions. Women managers are especially few and far between: in a survey of employers in South Wales, 50 percent reported that they had no women managers at all. The lack of women in top grades in education and training, as teachers and administrators, is also of concern as women in these positions perform mentoring, role model and networking functions.

- Self-employment and small businesses are important features of the Welsh economy, especially in rural areas: 8 percent of white women in Wales are self-employed, (a higher figure than in either England or Scotland). Self-employment is twice as high among women from ethnic minorities, and is particularly high among Pakistani and Chinese women. The EC-funded Athena project on women entrepreneurs in Wales uncovered major problems facing women wanting to set up in business. Enterprise agencies were not geared to women's needs or those of family businesses; training was often inappropriate.

PATTERNS AND RECENT TRENDS: A REVIEW OF STATISTICS

Patterns of participation

Women's participation in education has improved and some routes of access and progression are now well trodden. There are still areas and routes however where women are under-represented. It is important to note that beyond patterns of participation, there are also issues of how women experience education and training in Wales.

16 - 18 year olds

- There has been a rapid increase in staying-on rates over the last five years, from half the 16 year-olds in 1989 to 70 percent in 1993. Women stay on in larger numbers, especially in rural counties. Of those who stay on in education at 16, approximately two-thirds of men and women then continue in full-time education up to age 18. For those who do not stay on, a declining number are entering Youth Training; of these, men are the majority.

- The job market for young people has collapsed, and there are now only tiny numbers of jobs for 16 year-old school leavers with a training element. In 1993, less than 2 percent of girls left school at 16 to go into a job incorporating planned training. Most alarmingly, research in South Glamorgan shows that about a fifth of 16 to 18 year-olds are, at any one time, not in education, training or employment: many of them 'disappear' altogether from the system.

- Welsh 16-18 year olds perform relatively badly compared with England. There is a significantly higher percentage who leave with no qualifications at all. At the other end of the spectrum, the proportion with two or more A levels is also low. However, women perform better in this regard than men. Inter-county comparisons show that Mid Glamorgan fares the worst.

Further and Higher Education

- Women are the majority of **FE** students. There is a pattern of more women enrolling in open and evening courses and more men in work-integrated programmes. Two thirds of 'released' students are men, but such places are now drying up. Women pursue the more academic courses while men study for BTecs and City and Guilds. Women are less likely to end up with qualifications as a result of their studies.

- Women are still outnumbered by men (47 percent) studying in **non-university higher education**. Men are more likely to follow sandwich and release courses. Enrolments have grown, but there is a strong gender separation by subject area, especially in maths, technology and computing. Education and medical-related courses attract many more women.

- Welsh women slightly outnumber Welsh men as **undergraduates** across UK universities as a whole. There are large numbers of men and women in business administration and social studies courses. There, as in non-university HE, women are found in education and medical related courses while men predominate in the sciences. There is a clear lack of women in science, technology and engineering - all growth areas. Welsh women are under-represented in these fields not simply in relation to Welsh women, but compared with women from other parts of Britain too.

- Women have made inroads in **postgraduate** education: by the end of 1992 they constituted 44 percent of such students from Wales. There is a high concentration in a few subjects: 75 percent of women are accounted for in three out of ten subject lines while 80 percent of men are in just four subjects. 35 percent of all women postgraduates are in education compared with 20 percent of men. Welsh women are again under-represented in engineering and technology compared with female postgraduates throughout the UK.

- The number of **access** students expanded ten-fold in Wales between 1988/9 and 1993/4. Such programmes are now widely available throughout FE and increasingly in HE. Three-quarters of access students go on to HE courses. Women are the majority of access students (58%). However, there is still the issue of **breadth** to be addressed, especially that of opening up access to science degrees.

- In the **Open University** (OU) in Wales, overall patterns of enrolment and subject choice align closely with those in conventional university programmes. 43 percent of OU students in Wales are women (1992). This form of distance learning is more successful in attracting older women (over 40 years) than older men. 60 percent of women OU students are in the arts and social sciences. "Male" subjects attract fewer women than "female" subjects attract men.

- Overall women from ethnic minorities comprise 3.3 percent of all full-time students in Wales although they only comprise 1.5 percent of total numbers of women in the country. This is partly because of overseas students attending higher education institutions. Participation is particularly high among 'Chinese and other' ethnic groups.

Women and teaching: initial training and college lecturers

- Women are found to predominate in initial teacher training in Wales in the BEd (79%) and are more than half of those taking the higher qualification, the Post Graduate Certificate in Education (PGCE) (60%).

- Women teachers and managers can be important role models especially in non-traditional areas. However, despite the preponderance of women students in teacher training, men comprise 80 percent of lecturers and senior staff in FE and non-university HE. In universities, 80 percent of teaching and research staff are men.

The percentage of women in top jobs in the universities in Wales is significantly lower even than the low figure in England.

Other education and training for adults

- National Targets for Education and Training aim to have 80 percent of young people with the equivalent of NVQ level 2 (at least 5 GCSE passes at Grades A - C by 1997) and 50 percent the equivalent of NVQ level 3 (2 or more A levels or the vocational equivalent by the year 2000). Wales lags behind other countries of the UK in the percentage attaining NTETs at the Foundation levels - the qualifications aimed at young people. For Level 3, Wales is behind all the English regions as well. The gender breakdowns are not available.

- It might be hoped that the relatively poor showing of young adults in Wales attaining NTETs would be compensated for by later job-related training by older adults. Unfortunately, Wales shows up badly in regional comparison here too, and women in Wales do particularly poorly. The incidence of job-related training is not only worse comparing women in Wales with women in all the British regions, but the gap between men and women is largest in Wales too. Only 37 percent of Career Development Loans in Wales went to women.

- Training for Work is the main form of publicly-sponsored training for the adult unemployed. The data are weak, but suggest that more men participate than women. Wales again does not compare well with other parts of Britain in terms of the percentages of trainees who achieve a vocational training qualification. Traditional choices and occupational segregation patterns are very marked. In 1991, women from ethnic minorities in Wales were more likely to be on government schemes than in Scotland or England, and twice as likely as white women.

Educational attainment of the adult population: high level qualifications

- Across all age groups, more men overall in Wales have degree-level qualifications, while women are the majority of those with 'sub-degree' level HE diplomas. The female disadvantage is particularly pronounced in Mid Glamorgan and Gwent. This underlines the importance of continuing education and training for women to make up for the legacy of historically low female participation rates in higher education. While some women from ethnic minorities are well qualified, in South Glamorgan, which

xi

records the highest numbers of black and ethnic minority women, qualification rates are below those of the white population.

Statistics and Monitoring

Accurate, usable statistics are vital for gender monitoring. They are the basis for assessing progress. They provide insights on the impact of different policies on differential take-up and completion rates and results should be fed into strategic decision-making and planning. The impetus to improve gender monitoring of statistics should be strengthened by the work of the the Welsh Education and Training Information Working Group chaired by the Welsh Office.

Gender monitoring through statistics is a multi-faceted operation with a number of key dimensions. While gender is a dimension for which education and training data are often collected, unlike courses in the Welsh language, and participation by ethnic origin and disability, these are often presented as raw data, which makes interpretation cumbersome. Where possible, data on gender should be shown in percentages as well as numbers so that distributions are clear.

Colleges and TECs range widely in what they collect and in their ability to extract data when requested. Some statistics are weak, there is considerable variation in systems of record-keeping used, and changes in organisations have produced discontinuities. In our survey, this applies with particular force to the TECs at present.

The following recommendations for the gender monitoring of statistics were identified:

- A major step forward would be a '**gender scorecard**' for education and training statistics, made up of a series of indicators. Progress can then be monitored. This way, specific gaps in the statistics can be identified which need to be filled: these include information on 16 to 18 year-olds not in education, employment or training, and data on drop outs, student/trainee destinations, completion rates and staffing.

- It would be helpful if **guidelines** on gender monitoring systems could be developed for providers. These should allow cross tabulation with other variables such as ethnic origin. These could also clarify why data collection is important to developing institutional strategy.

- It is essential to develop an **integrated data management system** to pool data on education and training in Wales. This will avoid duplication of effort and the emergence of incompatible datasets. It will facilitate the development of strategic approaches towards training women. Welsh Office initiatives in the field of training statistics could prove very useful in this regard.

- Qualitative research is needed to follow up issues of women's training that cannot be reached through statistics. This would tap into women's **experience** of education and training, especially in male-dominated subjects. The impact of women-only training, including trainers, guidance and counselling could usefully be fed into strategic thinking on women and training.

- A **consortium approach** to the development of gender monitoring statistics is manageable at the level of Wales and would yield invaluable results. As training needs to be integrated into labour market and economic development policies more generally, this data would be of use to clienteles well beyond education and training providers and TECs.

EDUCATION AND TRAINING INITIATIVES

The EOC recently published *Realising Potential*, which identified education and training initiatives for women in Wales and brought out key points on good practice. We sought to avoid duplicating that publication, and focused only on selected examples of particular interest.

The Initiatives

- The role of **Chwarae Teg** in promoting women's training among employers has been vital. It has emphasised how strong is the business case for childcare, and has developed partnerships between employers and training providers towards better childcare.

- **South Glamorgan Women's Workshop** has won many awards for its pioneering work. It has an on-site nursery, charges no fees, and provides training for the disadvantaged in electronics and computing. New courses have been launched in telematics and telecommunications. Black and ethnic minority women, together with single parents, have been especially targeted.

xiii

- In an initiative which has received considerable coverage in the British press, the **Community University of the Valleys** brings higher education to the doorstep of people in a deprived South Wales Valley who lack access to transport. The biggest take up has been from women, the majority of whom had left school at 15 or 16.

- The **University of Wales College of Cardiff Bilingual Skills Training Project** creates an opportunity for bilingual women from ethnic minorities to improve their employment prospects by developing their translating and interpreting skills.

- There are seven EC funded **NOW** projects in Wales, and six members of **IRIS**, the EC funded network of women's training projects. They include projects in Dyfed, Clwyd, Gwent and Powys.

Lessons from Women's Education and Training Initiatives

These and many other initiatives tend to be started **by women for women**, in recognition of the gaps or inappropriateness of mainstream provision. The importance and effectiveness of **collaborative working** is demonstrated by many of these initiatives. The important point is to sustain these initiatives, while seeking to **mainstream** elements of good practice. The projects are invariably **funded on a shoe string**, with major energies being diverted from training to seeking further funding. More permanent funding is thus needed for many of these projects, as well as more advice and support for fund-seekers, especially as regards funding from the European Commission.

- The importance of **outreach work** is underlined, particularly for women in rural areas, single parents, women from ethnic minorities, women returners and some Welsh-speaking women. Employing women in outreach who share these characteristics is helpful.

- Lack of **childcare facilities** is a major barrier to the take-up of mainstream training. Childcare considerations affect the timing of courses, and suggest the need to develop innovative distance learning and other flexible arrangements for education and training.

- **Confidence-building** is essential, especially for women to move into male-dominated areas of education, training or work.

- Long term **guidance and counselling** is vital: the EC has recognised this in its planning for the new programmes, LEONARDO and SOCRATES.

- **Flexible systems** are needed with better developed routes of progression, modular units available allowing credit accumulation and transfer, and more points of entry to education and training systems.

- Many more women should be employed as senior teachers, trainers and managers in FE/HE institutions, thus offering **role models** to students.

- **Women-only training** works, especially in the field of new technologies; many more opportunities are needed.

CONCLUSIONS AND POLICY IMPLICATIONS

While there have been many signs of progress, the position of women in education and training in Wales remains worse in many respects than it is for men; it is even worse than for women in other parts of the UK. The picture is complex, but the main message from the review of research and the analysis of statistics is that equal treatment does not automatically result in equal outcome. Much existing provision is simply not in effect open to women. While there have been a large number of excellent initiatives, usually started by women to provide women-friendly training, they are peripheral to mainstream provision and cannot reach everyone.

Education and training systems are highly segregated by gender. Men predominate in scientific and engineering courses and those that have direct labour market links. Women make up large numbers of those in lower level FE and HE, and programmes not leading to qualifications. They lag well behind in vocational qualifications. Their qualifications are frequently not translated into labour market opportunities. The need of women for frequent career breaks and the drive for credentialism means that women returners will continue to face increasing difficulties reintegrating into the labour market unless provision for returners is improved.

General Policy Implications

- The first, and most important, is that **developing women's skills is essential to the development of the Welsh economy.** It is vital therefore that training policies be integrated with regional economic development strategies. The policy context provides a valuable opportunity to put the issue of women's education and training needs, and the needs of the economy for the development of women's skills, high on the agenda.

- Secondly, given the enduring pattern of gender segregation in education, training and employment, there is an obvious need for a new programme of effective **lifelong careers advice**. Promoting this now is timely, given the current reorganisation of the careers service, as well as the growing importance attached to guidance and counselling by the EC. This should address the stereotyped choices and low aspirations of school girls, the needs of unemployed women and returners, and the career development of employees. The potential of mentoring arrangements, networks and role models is extensive and needs to be explored effectively, given the desperate shortage of women in senior posts.

- Comprehensive gender monitoring through **education and training statistics** has a vital role to play; the results should feed into strategic thinking. This is as true for organisations involved in education and training provision as it is for the system as a whole at a regional and national levels. The focus needs to move forward from realising formal equality of access to identifying barriers to genuine equality of access. There are still outstanding gaps in the statistics, especially on student/trainee drop-out, completion, destination and on staffing. **Guidelines for education and training providers** on how to monitor, what to collect and how to present and use relevant data would be helpful.

- The **partnership** approach already successfully developed in Wales through Chwarae Teg and other consortia is a source of great strength in making progress, developing working relationships and developing awareness and a common culture. **Childcare** is a key issue which Chwarae Teg has approached through partnerships between colleges and employers: this will hopefully be emulated.

Research Priorities and Questions for the Future
- **Research** is needed on the qualitative experience of education and training by women, so that lessons in good practice can be mainstreamed. Major gaps in knowledge also exist on the experiences of young women after school not in education, training or employment; the reasons for the low level of women in decision making in Wales and

its impact particularly in education; and the low rates of employer-sponsored job-related training for women in Wales. Finally, access to Welsh medium education and training opportunities needs further documentation and exploration.

- The position of women in employer-sponsored training is especially problematic for women in Wales. This gives rise to the following questions: is it because women are not in those technical and managerial posts which tend to be targeted for training; or because of employers' attitudes or women's inability to manage education on top of family responsibilities; or is it that women are more likely to work in small and medium-sized enterprise which on the whole are less likely to offer training? Clearly employers need to review the criteria by which they select staff for training opportunities and consider how domestic, work and training commitments can be accommodated creatively.

- Given the increased focus on developing women's skills in the EC, it is vital to ensure that applications take advantage of opportunities of securing funding for training women effectively.

- There is a legacy of women who missed out on education first time round, whose skills need to be developed to participate in the workforce between now and the end of the century. Financial systems need to take this on board; it needs to be recognised that cuts in maintenance grants will impact particularly on women because they are less likely to get employer sponsorship, career loans and are likely to have responsibility for dependents. The role of the FEFCW and HEFCW is vital here to ensure the maintenance of the level of access funds which supplement the maintenance grants for women with particular needs. Colleges need their own childcare facilities for women with children to have better access to higher and further education.

- Finally, mainstreaming good practice from the many excellent initiatives in women's education and training must be the long term goal. Their successful and innovative features have general application, including attention to flexibility, modularisation, childcare, guidance and counselling, family-friendy hours, confidence-building, affordable fees, routes of progression, and women-only training where appropriate. Developing the economy of Wales relies particularly upon developing the skills of its women, to date an under-used national resource.

1. INTRODUCTION

The Equal Opportunities Commission (EOC) commissioned this study to:

> examine the current situation of women and men within education and training
> in Wales and to assess the policy initiatives which have already been undertaken
> in this area. Mechanisms to monitor and evaluate ongoing processes within
> education and training can also be established.

The study is part of the EOC's contribution to the work of Chwarae Teg in Wales (Chwarae Teg is Welsh for 'fair play'). Chwarae Teg is an independent consortium of organisations which includes the Welsh Development Agency (WDA), Training and Enterprise Councils (TECs), local authorities and the EOC itself which is seeking to expand the role of women in the workforce. One of the main strategies of Chwarae Teg is to develop women's access to and participation in training. It has recently received funding from the Welsh Office for some of its activities. Fair Play, an initiative modelled on Chwarae Teg, has now been launched by the Secretary of State for Employment together with the EOC in the English regions. However, it is to be co-ordinated from the Employment Department, unlike Chwarae Teg which is independent.

The aims and objectives of the study are:

(i) to give an account of *context* by:

- describing the policy setting; and
- outlining the position of women in the labour market.

(ii) to provide a *statistical review of the position of women in education and training* by:

- mapping statistically the position of women in education and training in Wales;
- reviewing the quality and quantity of gender monitoring statistics in education and training; and
- making recommendations about gaps in the statistical base and the development of gender monitoring systems.

(iii) to analyse *special initiatives* oriented towards women in education and training by:

- conducting a literature search;
- drawing lessons from the patterns of initiatives;
- making recommendations for further work on examining initiatives in greater depth, and monitoring education and training issues on an ongoing basis.

The study is particularly timely as the policy context has undergone dramatic change recently. The devolution of responsibility for education and training in Wales to the Welsh Office, the seven Welsh TECs and the Higher and Further Education Funding Councils for Wales, over a relatively short space of time, has created opportunities for strategic policy development responsive to the needs of Wales.

At the same time there is a trend towards the 'marketisation' of education and training, and it is important that any implied deregulation does not mean that equal opportunities and women's needs are afforded a low priority. Labour market and demographic changes mean that it is increasingly important to ensure that women's skills are developed to their full potential.

Wales is characterised by low (but rising) female economic activity rates and low-skilled female jobs, many of which are part-time and poorly paid compared with those in English regions. Although there have been significant improvements in women's participation in education and training, this has not been translated into labour market opportunities. Patterns of gender segregation in the Welsh labour force are particularly marked, and there is a dearth of women in top jobs.

Despite this, there has been a wide range of initiatives aimed at developing women's skills, many started by women themselves. There are key lessons to be learned from these initiatives; the challenge is to mainstream good practice.

The study was very limited in time and resources, so essentially secondary sources had to be relied upon for the review of policy, context and special initiatives, together with semi-structured interviews with a few key actors. Academic studies, published reports and some unpublished documents were drawn upon.

The statistical mapping of the position of women in education and training drew upon both published statistics and a survey of all the further education (FE) colleges and TECs. The analysis of existing data revealed that many published figures, such as the welcome new series **Further and Higher Education and Training Statistics in Wales** (Welsh Office 1993a, 1994a) are not presented in such a way as to make the gender dimension clear: considerable secondary analysis of raw data is required. The survey of FE colleges and TECs revealed that there are no systematic patterns of record-keeping: the ability to respond to our requests for information on women's participation patterns varied widely.

Appendix III presents statistical material which comprises a secondary analysis of both published data, and unpublished data kindly provided for us by bodies included in the list in Appendix I. We are most grateful for the time they took to provide us with the information we requested.

The study drew upon the expertise of members of the project steering committee and the Chwarae Teg Training and Education Network Working Group (which is jointly sponsored by EOC Wales and the National Institute of Adult and Continuing Education (NIACE) Wales Committee). The high profile of EOC Wales in the Principality was most beneficial to the study and undoubtedly boosted response to requests for information.

The results of the study show that, while the position of women in education and training in Wales compares unfavourably with the rest of Britain, there has been great progress in the last ten years. Participation rates have improved overall, although gender-stereotyping subject choices remain an important feature. South Glamorgan Women's Workshop, an internationally acclaimed initiative which targets disadvantaged women for training, particularly black and ethnic minority women, has recently celebrated its tenth anniversary. Access courses have mushroomed, and the main beneficiaries are women. There are more courses targetting women returners and taking on board important issues that pose barriers to women's participation such as childcare needs, confidence-building, and guidance.

The report shows that despite this progress, there is an urgent need for a more systematic approach to women's education and training needs in Wales, both for economic reasons – to ensure that Wales does not become a low-skill, low-wage region of Europe – and in order to combat discrimination. The final chapter identifies policy implications and research priorities derived from the review. It makes recommendations on gender monitoring of statistics, and raises some questions for the future.

2. THE POLICY CONTEXT

2.1 INTRODUCTION

This chapter reviews some of the major features of the policy context for the study. Education and training have undergone major changes in the last five years at both the UK level and more particularly within Wales itself. Significant shifts have occurred in the roles of organisations with responsibilities for education and training: there has been considerable devolution from Whitehall to Wales.

The new *roles and responsibilities* for education and training in Wales have been accompanied by the development of consortia and partnerships within Wales. Chwarae Teg acted as a catalyst to projects being developed by members of its consortium, focusing on women's training needs. Opportunity 2000 has enlisted companies in developing the role of women in the workforce. Other partnerships and consortia have emerged.

At the same time, there is a trend towards the *marketisation* of education and training. Formula funding means that some adult education courses which have served women well may be unprofitable. The provision of childcare may not be regarded as cost-effective. Courses for women returners, which may need elements of confidence-building and may not net the same end results in terms of qualification rates as courses for other groups, become less 'economic'. Outreach work, and provision for those women from ethnic minorities with language needs are not as lucrative as other courses. The net effect of marketisation on women's education and training is difficult to predict overall: women have proved to be keen consumers, but the effect of the formulae may restrict the provision of suitable opportunities for them.

Finally, a major source of funding for training in Wales is the *European Commission (EC)*. The EC is increasingly concerned about the need to develop women's skills. This is for both economic reasons (given demographic changes and skill shortages in the European Union) and social reasons (the need to avoid large-scale social exclusion of women). Attempts are being made to ensure that women's needs are in future mainstreamed in the European Social Fund (ESF). The EC's Task Force Human Resources, Education, Training and Youth, is about to launch a new training programme, LEONARDO DA VINCI, and a new education programme, SOCRATES, which will incorporate many of the features of earlier programmes, but have more emphasis on developing women's skills. NOW (New Opportunities for Women), the EC initiative specifically on women's training, is about to begin a new six-year phase with twice the former budget. IRIS, the network of women's training projects in Europe, has just begun a second, expanded phase.

These three themes of roles and responsibilities, marketisation and the European Commission provide the organising structure for this chapter. It is not intended to be a comprehensive account of the policy context, but identifies some of the key factors. Given the rate of change in recent years however, a full account of the organisations and their roles would nevertheless be a useful document for the ever-increasing number of actors in the field.

2.2   ROLES AND RESPONSIBILITIES: PARTNERS AND CONSORTIA

The field of post-compulsory education and training has seen major policy changes in the last five years which have been reflected in different institutional arrangements, curricula and delivery mechanisms.

Creditation is now a key element and new qualifications such as National Vocational Qualifications (NVQs), and targets for training – the National Targets for Education and Training (NTETs), formerly the National Education and Training Targets (NETTs) – have been established.

A second major feature has been the devolution of responsibility for training. The Welsh Office is now accountable for further education (FE), higher education (HE) and training within Wales, and seven locally-based TECs have been set up in the Principality. The ending of local authority control of FE has led to many college mergers and growing independence of individual institutions. Responsibility for funding has been devolved to the Higher Education Funding Council for Wales (HEFCW) and Further Education Funding Council for Wales (FEFCW) respectively. The end of the trans-binary divide has meant that, in addition to the six colleges of the University of Wales, there is the new University of Glamorgan. The Welsh Development Agency (WDA) has a keen interest in skills development, given its role in developing the economy and attracting inward investment. In addition to statutory bodies, many other organisations are playing an increasingly important role in education and training, for example *Fforwm*, which brings together FE colleges in Wales, the Council of TECs in Wales, and the National Institute of Adult and Continuing Education in Wales Committee.

A number of partnerships and consortia have emerged. The Welsh Office has brought together representatives of TECs, colleges and other organisations into the Welsh Education and Training Information Working Group (WETIWG) to consider jointly the information requirements of the training and post-16 education sectors, agree common definitions for databases and consider common research and information projects and surveys. Through development of common frameworks, the participation of women in education and training in Wales will be much more visible in the future.

The Welsh TECs jointly fund their own co-ordinator. Organisations in Wales can draw upon the services of a largely WDA sponsored Wales European Centre in Brussels.

However, for our purposes, two of the most interesting developments are Chwarae Teg, the consortium of partners which developed an action plan to improve the role of women in the Welsh workforce, and Opportunity 2000, launched a year later in Wales than in England and with 30 subscribing employers as members. This section gives a brief description of the role of the Welsh Office and the TECs, and these two partnerships which focus on women's training needs. The EOC plays a major role in many of these partnership arrangements.

The Welsh Office
Now that the Welsh Office has taken over responsibility for the Careers Service and FE, HE and training in Wales, it has the potential to develop a co-ordinated approach. Unlike English regions, these functions are concentrated in the one government department. The new Integrated Regional Offices in England will in the future have some of the same scope for developing a co-ordinated approach already available in Wales and in Scotland.

The former Training Education and Enterprise Department (TEED) – now the Industry and Training Department (ITD) – of the Welsh Office produced a consultation document on training, education and enterprise: **People and Prosperity: A Challenge to Wales** (Welsh Office 1993b). This sets out a framework for the development of a coherent strategy. The document specifically identifies a number of areas where action is needed to develop the potential of women in the workforce. Views are solicited on identifying the best way to ensure that equal opportunities are promoted by all agencies in contact with employers to counteract gender-stereotyped career choices by young people, to identify specific targets for women in relation to the NTETs, to provide women with access to effective training, and to support the business needs of women entrepreneurs.

The document has provoked a wide response from individuals and organisations, and these responses are currently being examined. The intention is then to develop a document late in 1994 which will set out strategic aims and action points for the organisations concerned. A key element of the strategy is likely to be a focus on developing an infrastructure to deliver quality training, and a flexible system of delivery.

A further policy development is the commitment to developing new style apprenticeships. This is taking place in Wales a year ahead of England and will focus on the engineering and manufacturing industries. The apprenticeships are likely to be shorter and more intensive than those largely discontinued in Britain over a decade ago, with more emphasis on quality.

Training and Enterprise Councils

The seven Welsh TECs' contracts require them to take equal opportunities seriously as an issue, but as yet the attention paid to it has been variable. However, six out of the seven TECs are contracting Chwarae Teg to undertake work in 1994/95 to meet equal opportunities targets, and all the TECs are now fully engaged in the Out of School Childcare Initiative which includes an investment in training. Not all TECs have an identifiable equal opportunities person which could either mean that the issue is mainstreamed, or that it is not tackled at all.

Welsh TECs were examined in the EOC's *Formal Investigation into the Publicly Funded Vocational Training System in England and Wales* (EOC 1993). Six of the seven TECs responded to an initial request for information, of which three had referred to equal opportunities in their corporate objectives, and four had drawn up equal opportunities policy statements.

Only one Welsh TEC referred at that time to the possible appointment of an equal opportunities development manager, compared with half the English TECs participating in the EOC study. All but one of the Welsh TECs are, however, members of the Chwarae Teg consortium which aims to enhance the role of women in the Welsh workforce (see below).

The gender distribution of boards is as one would expect: there are no women chairs of boards and very few women TEC board members. As in England, this is in part a consequence of the regulations governing the selection of board members; they must be in senior positions already and fewer women satisfy that criterion than men. There is awareness of this problem and the Secretary of State for Wales has agreed that the regulations concerning selection of board members should be looked at again within the Welsh Office.

There are currently no women chief executives, and few women in senior positions within TECs. It is important to monitor the position of women in organisations while at the same time not expecting them to deliver equal opportunities single-handedly themselves: that requires commitment throughout the organisation.

The report of the **Formal Investigation** made a number of recommendations which hopefully will be taken up by the TECs. These include the development of an equal opportunities strategy, with assistance from the Welsh Office, the inclusion of equal opportunities issues in annual strategies and planning guides, the development of an equal opportunities network, encouragement to TECs to join the EOC's Equality Exchange, and more monitoring of statistics. Many of those recommendations are reinforced in this report.

Chwarae Teg

Chwarae Teg was launched in 1992 in South Wales and extended to North, Mid and West Wales in 1993. It comprises six of the seven TECs, the EOC, the WDA, the Development Board for Rural Wales, the Employment Service, the National Health Service in Wales, and county and district councils.

Core funding has been provided by the Welsh Office with effect from 1 April 1994, which will help it to extend its activities. The four main foci of Chwarae Teg's Action Plan activities have been: increasing awareness of women's potential, childcare, seeking to ensure that training courses are more accessible and meet the needs of women better, and developing flexible hours.

Chwarae Teg has played an important role in increasing awareness of the underutilisation of women in the workforce. It co-ordinates the members of the consortium to work on joint projects. One such initiative was the WDA funded study **Expanding the Role of Women in the Workforce** (C. Rees and Willox 1991a; Willox and Virgin 1991, 1992) which included surveys of employers. Its publications on the business case for childcare have been particularly important given the recent findings of a study of the economically inactive in Wales, in which women reported that lack of childcare facilities was a major barrier to the return to work (ERES 1994). Linked with childcare needs are training needs, again particularly of women returners.

David Hunt, the then Secretary of State for Employment and erstwhile Secretary of State for Wales announced in spring 1994 that regional consortia, called Fair Play and modelled on Chwarae Teg, will be set up in the English regions, in line with the new Integrated Regional Offices. They will however be run from the regional offices of the Employment Department, whereas Chwarae Teg remains independent.

Opportunity 2000

Opportunity 2000 is a national campaign to increase the quality and quantity of women's participation in the workforce. It was launched by Business in the Community in November 1991, with support from the Prime Minister, John Major. Opportunity 2000 was set up in Wales in 1992. Although only 30 employers in Wales subscribe, Business in the Community has calculated that one-fifth of the Welsh labour force works for organisations committed to the aims of Opportunity 2000.

The Opportunity campaign centres on five main areas: training and development programmes; creating a family-friendly workplace; recruitment, selection and promotion procedures; communication of goals, action plans and progress and changing organisational structure.

The main thrust of the campaign in Wales is no longer recruitment but consolidation. Opportunity 2000 is now working with Chwarae Teg to a common action plan and producing a joint newsletter. They will be collaborating on workshops on flexible working in 1995.

2.3 THE MARKETISATION OF PUBLIC POST-COMPULSORY EDUCATION AND TRAINING

The term 'marketisation' in relation to post-compulsory education and training may be clumsy but it is accurate. The tenor of policies over recent years has been to introduce increasing elements of competition and market structures. The underlying rationale is that this encourages competitive efficiency with providers of education and training having to respond to individual demand, rather than furthering their own institutional interests (for a general discussion of this major trend in public policy, and the issues it raises, see Le Grand and Bartlett 1993).

This is not the place to engage in a critique of these policies as our interest is in equal opportunities specifically. It must be noted on the positive side, nevertheless, that training policies have received greater attention and priority over the past five years than they did before, and that this is no mean achievement. Yet it is also necessary to note the caution expressed by the detractors of marketisation. They maintain either that market mechanisms do not automatically bring efficiency (and may indeed lead to substantial duplication of effort by each institution), or that responding to individual demands is not always the preferable course in seeking to realise such long-term aims as fostering economic development or equality of opportunity in Wales.

Evidence of 'marketisation' is substantial. There is now fierce competition between secondary schools and further education colleges for individual enrolments as funding has come to be tied directly to student numbers. Schools have made substantial advances in vocational provision, where there is no long tradition, in direct competition with the colleges. The 'incorporation' of the FE colleges also came into effect in 1993, whereby each college is now free-standing, with its own board and budget, rather than under the control of local government. Many in management in the FE sector welcome the autonomy, though how much so is strongly related to the relationships previously enjoyed with the Local Education Authority (LEA); where this was collaborative rather than controlling in the past there is less that is new. FE lecturers are already acutely aware of the impact of the incorporation referred to above on contracts and conditions. The point here is 'marketisation': colleges control their own budgets, they are dependent for their funding on the FEFCW using formulae based on student numbers, and on their TEC for a section of their budget for work-related FE, and are set in competition one with another.

Training Credits, directing funds to individual young people for them to spend with providers that they choose, are being much more widely introduced in Wales in 1994. 'A training credit is a voucher showing a money value ... put in the hands of young people leaving full-time education at 16 or 17. It entitles them to vocational education and training, and buys them the opportunity to qualify with a National Vocational Qualification at NVQ Level 2 (or its equivalent) or higher' (Department of Education and Science/Department of the Environment/Welsh Office 1991, p. 34). They strengthen the links still more between individual enrolments in education or training and funding to the provider (hence 'marketisation'); this despite some scepticism in the field that pilot credit schemes have proved their value. The careers services are to be put out to tender; from 1995, they will cease to operate under LEA auspices as they do at present and may be operated by partnerships or even private organisations depending on success in the process of tendering.

At the all-Wales level, the Funding Councils have been established in the wake of the demise of the LEAs. That Wales has its own Councils may well mean that they are more sensitive to local needs and offer a less distant service than their counterparts in England. But, as regards FE for example, the newly established Council officially has no planning role which means that it is primarily concerned with administration and the efficient disbursement of funds. A key player remains the Welsh Office but, given these market-oriented reforms, planning roles are not clearly defined. It is also too soon to assess the extent of co-ordination that will be undertaken by *Fforwm*, the association of colleges newly established in Wales post-incorporation with a view to providing a collective voice in the otherwise decentralised organisations described in this section. The point to underline here is that with less explicit planning, with faith placed instead on the operation of education and training markets, planning for equal opportunities may also be 'off limits'. Much depends on the extent to which patterns of student and trainee enrolment and participation reflecting equal opportunities will in the future enter explicitly into the funding formulae that now drive the system.

In HE, problems as regards women and equal opportunities may arise from the 'two-tier' (or multi-tier) system that is being created – between research-rich and research-poor institutions, and between faculties that attract more substantial per capita funding and the cheaper and over-subscribed programmes in arts and humanities (programmes catering for many women HE students) – as part of the larger approach to competition and governance. These developments may well affect especially the quality of the higher education that many women receive.

Bringing together these different trends towards marketisation, there is no doubt that, after years of serious neglect, publicly-sponsored training is receiving more of the attention it deserves. In recent years, legislation and reforms have been plentiful but, despite the progress represented by such attention, this in itself is a cause for concern. For there is a tendency to embark on 'all-change', rather than build on achievements. The danger is that this will apply to women's initiatives just as it does in other aspects of training. The TECs, until so recently the flagships of government training policy, are the latest bodies to come in for severe scrutiny, and major changes over the next five years in Wales are now conceivable. It is not just that such constant change alters the context of realising equal opportunities; it is also that all the experience and contacts on women's issues built up within such organisations may be lost with each shake-up.

11

From the viewpoint of equal opportunities, the impact of all this is unclear. It is quite possible that responsiveness to individual demands means *ipso facto* responsiveness to the demands of women – as workers, as learners, as parents (or all at the same time). The fact that many of the jobs that are being created in Wales are taken by women might also mean that training linked to these implies that women will benefit (though the evidence reviewed in later chapters does not suggest that that demand is burgeoning).

But there are also less sanguine interpretations of these changes and some of these have already been rehearsed. Many 'unprofitable' programmes, for instance in adult education which have traditionally served so many women in Wales, are no longer viable. Most of all there is a need to review the nature of policy planning, and to consider where this leaves the treatment of equal opportunities issues. Specifically, the question arises, what are the mechanisms through which deficiencies can be made good, even though that might mean that markets are 'bucked' or that individuals' choices cease to be the paramount guides to educational investment?.

2.4   WOMEN AND TRAINING: THE EUROPEAN POLICY CONTEXT

The European Commission (EC) has emphasised that the development of the skills in the European Union (EU) is an important part of its current economic development policy to enhance the economic competitiveness of the European Union's workforce, as spelled out in the White Paper **Growth, Competitiveness, Employment: The Challenges and Ways Forward into the 21st Century** (Commission of the European Communities 1993a). At the same time, the Green Paper **European Social Policy: Options for the Future** (Commission of the European Communities 1993b) stresses that women's skills need to be enhanced if they are to avoid social exclusion through unemployment, underemployment and poverty. As a consequence, applicants for funding for training from the EC may need to pay more attention to their equal opportunities objectives in the future.

European Commission support for training from the Commission of the European Union comes from two main sources: the matched funding provided by the Directorate General for Employment and Social Affairs' European Social Fund (ESF), and that for innovative projects under the programmes run by the Task Force Human Resources Education, Training and Youth – COMETT, FORCE, ERASMUS, PETRA, YOUTH FOR EUROPE, IRIS, LINGUA, TEMPUS and EUROTECNET (see Table 2.1). The COMETT programme has a regional network of offices,

University Enterprise Training Partnerships (UETPs) to assist local companies and education institutions to develop applications. In Wales, there are two UETPS, the main one being Gateway Europe based in the WDA Skills Development Offices in the Treforest Industrial Estate outside Cardiff. It has been very effective in developing an understanding of EC funding amongst partners in Wales.

Table 2.1   **EC task force education and training programmes, 1986–93**

Short title	Full title	Duration	Budget execution up to 1992 (ECUm)
COMETT	Programme on co-operation between universities and industry regarding training in the field of technology	1986–94	206.6
ERASMUS	EC action scheme for the mobility of university students	1987–	307.5
PETRA	Action programme for the vocational training of young people and their preparation for adult working life	1988–94	79.7
YOUTH FOR EUROPE	Action programme for the promotion of youth exchanges in the Community – 'Youth for Europe' programme	1988–94	32.2
IRIS	European network of vocational training projects for women	1988–93	0.75
EUROTECNET	Action programme to promote innovation in the field of vocational training resulting from technological change in the EC	1990–94	7.0
LINGUA	Action programme to promote foreign language competence in the EC	1990–94	68.8
TEMPUS	Trans-European mobility scheme for university studies	1990–94	194.0
FORCE	Action programme for the development of continuing vocational training in the EC	1991–94	31.3

Source: Commission of the European Communities (1993d).

The ESF is mainly used in Britain to subsidise Employment Department programmes for the unemployed. It is administered by TECs (and in Scotland by Local Enterprise Companies – LECs). However, under the NOW programme, funds have been accessed for women's training in Wales, for example training in management at University College, Swansea, and training in telecommunications and telematics in South Glamorgan Women's Workshop (see Chapter 3 for a full account of NOW projects in Wales). Figures on the participation of women in ESF-funded programmes in Wales appear in Table 2.2.

Table 2.2 Projects in Wales approved under ESF Objective 3, measure 331[1] and Objective 4, measure 431,[2] 1993

Project	ESF approved (£)	Trainees (N)
Measure 331		
Women into business	40,770	30
Women returners – IT	67,716	40
Women and computers	27,588	260
Women in technology	48,056	120
Women into work	8,761	24
Technology and business skills	37,714	44
Women into technology	4,581	12
New technology training	68,102	128
New technology and business skills	37,689	45
Measure 431		
Young women into business	13,334	10
Engineering, science and information technology	13,714	16
New technology training	17,059	34

Note: [1] Training for long-term unemployed (more than 1 year).
[2] Training for young (less than 25 years) unemployed women in non-traditional occupations.

Source: Assembly of Welsh Counties.

A study on women's participation in Task Force programmes commissioned by the Task Force revealed that women appeared in about equal numbers in the projects aimed at young people such as such PETRA, or those geared towards languages such as LINGUA, but are found relatively rarely in the more expensive technological training programmes such as FORCE and COMETT (T. Rees 1993a). The net effect then is that the programmes are in danger of further polarising the skill levels of men and women. The lesson here is that equal access does not ensure equal outcome, and that a *laissez-faire* approach to equal opportunities in training can widen the skills gap between men and women. This point is borne out in the discussion in later chapters on the pattern of participation of men and women in education and training in Wales.

The Task Force programmes are all due to end in December 1994. LEONARDO DA VINCI and SOCRATES are still in the design stage and are not due to begin until January 1995 following approval by the European Parliament and the Council of Ministers. However, the Commission is seeking to ensure that the new programmes are designed to accommodate women's training needs more directly than their predecessors.

This is being done though measures that 'tinker' with the system (improving equality of access through enhanced gender monitoring, equal opportunities statements, etc.), 'tailor' the system (positive action measures such as earmarked budgets for women's training, confidence-building, women-only training), and 'transforming' the system (redesigning provision to meet a more diverse range of needs and circumstances) (T. Rees 1993a, 1994d). This is clearly of some importance to education and training providers in Wales.

One component of the Task Force strategy has been the development of project ALPHA to train staff of UETPs, including those in Wales, in equal opportunities. The purpose has been both to raise awareness among UETP staff, and also to facilitate them to raise pertinent questions when assisting applicants for Task Force funding, and help them to formulate equal opportunities objectives in their bids. In this way the Commission is seeking to act as a catalyst to increase awareness of the need for developing equal opportunities in training at grass roots level within the Member States.

The new emphasis on women's education and training needs has been reinforced by the publication of a report entitled **Social Partners' Joint Opinion on Women and Training** by the Commission of the European Communities (1993c). The Social Partners at European level are the Union of Industrial and Employers' Confederations of Europe – UNICE; European Centre of Enterprises with Public Participation – CEEP; and the European Trade Union Confederation – ETUC. CEC 1993c). The Social Partners are reinforcing this by compiling a **Compendium of Good Practice in Training for Women** with funding from the European Commission. This compendium will be disseminated widely through trade unions' and employers' organisations and through UETPs and government departments. It should provide models which training providers and companies in Wales will be able to follow in the future for initial, intermediate and continuing training.

Within Wales, it is interesting to note that women have been particularly active in the organisations concerned with accessing funds for training from Europe, within the Wales European Centre in Brussels, in Gateway Europe, and in various key positions in local authorities and Welsh TECs. Women make up on average between 30 and 45 per cent of participants at Gateway conferences on Task Force programmes, with the exception of the Athena conference on women's skills where they constituted 86 per cent of attendees (figures supplied by Gateway Europe). The strength of the female Welsh network was particularly visible at the IRIS Fair, **Women: A Vital Resource,** held in Brussels in October 1992 (as witnessed in photographs which later appeared in Gateway Europe's newsletter).

The implications for women of the White Paper on economic growth are currently being examined in Brussels. There are attempts to 'feminise the mainstream' of Task Force programmes. This new emphasis on women's training needs at the European level creates an opportunity for organisations within Wales to address the issue more directly.

2.5   CONCLUSION

In conclusion, the policy context is one of considerable recent and impending changes. Three major trends are the development of all-Wales partnerships, the marketisation of education and training, and an increased interest in women's training needs from the EC, a major funder. There is an urgent need to ensure that equal opportunities generally and women's needs in particular are kept centre-stage in the development of new policies. It is especially important to ensure that the bottlenecks and barriers facing women are addressed in the formula system, and that EC funding is accessed appropriately.

3. WOMEN AND THE LABOUR MARKET IN WALES

3.1 INTRODUCTION

This section provides a brief overview of the context of the study by describing the position of women in the labour market in Wales, and reviewing recent relevant research. It illustrates that Wales is characterised by a particularly low rate of female economic activity (although this has been rising in recent years) and that women in the workforce tend to be in relatively low-paid, low-skilled and often part-time employment. There are proportionately fewer women in top jobs, compared with England. This chapter draws upon a range of available secondary sources, including academic research, government reports, and published reports. Coverage is patchy: some aspects are better documented that others. Major studies of note include the WDA study **Expanding the Role of Women in the Workforce in North and South Wales** (C. Rees and Willox 1991a; Willox and Virgin 1992), an Economic and Social Research Council funded study of 30 employers' recruitment and training policies in the Bridgend Travel to Work Area (G. Rees and Fielder 1992; G. Rees et al. 1991), and work commissioned by the (as was) Training Agency on women and the demand for and supply of information technology skills in South East Wales (G. Rees et al. 1989; T Rees 1994b).

The chapter begins with a brief account of key characteristics of women in the labour force. Various groups of women with different education and training needs are the focus of the main body of the chapter, which begins by examining secondary schoolgirls' occupational and career choices. Although compulsory education is outside the remit of this report, schoolgirls' very limited options and occupational choices will have an impact upon adult women's training needs in the near future.

The key issues identified in this chapter are that women's economic activity rates in Wales are very low, and that women are clustered in a narrow range of industries and at the bottom of the tier in those industries. Moreover education and training systems are highly segregated by gender. Far more flexible training and more open patterns of employment are needed to break the stranglehold of gender as a determinant of education, training and occupational lifechances.

3.2 KEY FEATURES OF THE LABOUR FORCE IN WALES

This section briefly identifies some of the key characteristics of the female Welsh labour force. Full accounts of the Welsh labour force and the economy can be found elsewhere, for example T. Rees

17

(1994a); Thomas (1992); Wales TUC (1994b); Welsh Office (1994b). For an overview of demographic changes in Wales and the growth of single parenthood, see Betts (1994).

Economic activity rates

Both male and female economic activity rates in Wales are low compared with the regions of England. Wales is currently characterised by a convergence of activity rates for men and women: those for men have been steadily declining over the last decade to the 1992 figure of 69 per cent, while those for women have been increasing to the 1992 level of 48 per cent (Labour Force Survey, Spring Quarter). This is linked to patterns of industrial restructuring where male dominated industries such as steel and coal have given way to service sector industries which employ women, particularly on a part-time basis.

The main reasons for women's inactivity have been identified in a survey of the economically inactive in Wales as poor health and caring responsibilities (ERES 1994). The number of permanently sick females of working age in Wales increased by 247.3 per cent compared with 171.3 per cent in England in the period 1981–91: women now comprise just over one-third of the 130,000 individuals of working age who are classified as permanently sick in Wales (ERES 1994, original source 1991 Census). Rates of sickness among women of working age are particularly high in Mid Glamorgan.

Women at home with children have been identified as the major source of new entrants to the British labour market between now and the end of the century (Metcalf and Leighton 1989). Many of these will have had their skills and confidence levels eroded as a consequence of having spent time out of the labour market. In Gwent, it has been calculated that as many as 9,000 people (of whom 60 per cent are women) currently outside the labour market are looking for work, while a further 20,000, mainly over age 24 (of whom 75 per cent are women), are likely to do so in the next five years (Gwent TEC 1993). The WDA studies, exploring the potential of expanding the role of women in the workforce found that while many women in both North and South Wales expressed satisfaction with their current position at home, most intended to return to work at some stage in the future (C. Rees and Willox 1991b; Willox and Virgin 1992). Welsh-speaking women appear to feature disproportionately among economically inactive women in North Wales.

Occupational segregation, part-time work and pay

The Welsh workforce is highly segregated, both horizontally and vertically, with women working in a narrow range of industries and in the lower grades within those sectors. They comprise over two-thirds of all workers in personal and protective services, clerical and secretarial, sales and 'other occupations'.

At the other end of the scale, as Table 3.1 shows, a study commissioned by HTV Wales revealed that there are very few women in top jobs in Wales (T. Rees and Fielder 1991; 1992; T. Rees 1994a). The situation compares badly with that in England, which was itself roundly condemned by the Hansard Society Commission (Hansard Society Commission on Women at the Top 1990).

Table 3.1   Women as a percentage of top grades in selected sectors in Wales, 1991

Sector	% women
Civil service (grades 1–4)	3.0
Local government (principal officers in county councils)	3.5
Solicitors (partners and single practitioners)	9.6
Company directors	2.3
University professors	1.3
Secondary school heads	6.9
Health Service consultants	13.3

Source: T. Rees and Fielder (1991).

The numbers of women in senior posts in the public and private sectors in Wales is minute, the proportion of women managers is much lower than in England and the proportion of women headteachers in Wales is actually declining (T. Rees and Fielder 1991, 1992; T. Rees 1994a). A recent survey of employers in South Wales revealed that 50 per cent of establishments had no women managers at all (C. Rees and Willox 1991a).

The lack of women in top grades more generally is of great concern as they can provide role models, perform a mentoring role and develop networks to encourage other women. This point is taken up again in Chapter 4 when we look specifically at women in FE and HE.

Women in Wales earn less than in Scotland and England, but the pay differential between men and women in Wales is not as great as male wages are so low relative to national averages. In 1993, Welsh women earned on average £231.60 per week (75 per cent of male earnings). This ranged from £177.90 for manual workers and £247.60 for non-manual women workers (Department of Employment 1993b).

The trend towards Wales becoming a low-wage economy is apparent in the figures for part-time women workers' pay. Women working part-time now constitute a quarter of the Welsh workforce. Such jobs are almost always low-paid, with few opportunities for training or promotion.

Childcare

Caring commitments were identified in the ERES survey of the economically inactive in Wales as a major deterrent to returning to the labour force (ERES 1994). Although these commitments include caring of various kinds (such as elderly relatives and permanently handicapped or sick children), the lack of affordable childcare facilities is a particular problem in Wales. State-provided childcare in the UK is amongst the worst in the EU, and the problem is exacerbated by the low wages of women in Wales.

The current level of childcare places compares unfavourably with that of England: seven places compared with ten per 100 children (1991 figures, Chwarae Teg 1993a). Some districts and counties fare better than others: provision is particularly poor in Dyfed at three places per 100 children, and where the female economic activity rate is the lowest of all Welsh counties. Chwarae Teg estimates (1993a, p. 52):

> A target growth of up to 40 per cent between 1991 and 1996 would be appropriate if childcare for the under fives is to meet the demand arising from the growth in women's employment and earnings expected for that period and to catch up with the 1991 figure for England.

Lack of childcare facilities is a particular problem for single parents (Malvisi et al. 1990; Chwarae Teg 1993a):

> Employment rates of lone parents (including men) are much lower than those of women in couples: 17 per cent of those with children under five and 45 per cent for those whose youngest child is over 5. This pattern is repeated in all districts but the differential between lone parents and those in couples is greatest in the

urban areas (e.g. Newport, Cardiff and Swansea).
(Chwarae Teg 1993a, original source 1991 Census)

Care in the community policies entail additional commitments for women, which again constrain their ability to engage in education, training and employment opportunities.

Welsh language

The 1991 Census shows that Welsh speaking has increased throughout the Principality over the last ten years. About 18 per cent of the total population reported themselves as being able to speak Welsh in the 1991 Census (Morris 1994), although a Welsh Office report estimates that approximately 38 per cent of the population have some knowledge of Welsh (Jones 1993). This includes figures as high as 61 per cent in the Welsh language heartland of North West Wales and 44 per cent in Dyfed. The age group with the highest proportion of Welsh speakers is now the 3–15 age group. This clearly has important implications for post-school education and training provision in the future. The spatial distribution of Welsh speaking among 3–15 year-olds by TEC area ranges considerably from for example 62.9 per cent in North West Wales to 30.7 per cent in West Wales, 30.0 per cent in Powys and 4.8 per cent in Gwent (North West Regional Research Laboratory 1993).

A study of 1991 Census data by Morris revealed that '… women born outside Wales are still the most prominent group within the upper echelons of the class structure' (Morris 1994, p. 25). Moreover:

> Welsh-speaking men appear to have a greater prominence than Welsh-speaking
> women at the top of the social class scale, but their position is still inferior to that
> of the non-Welsh born men at the top.

The study shows that a higher percentage of Welsh-speaking women are either unemployed or have not had a job outside the home for ten or more years.

Welsh-speaking women are under-represented among those who return to learning in institutes of higher education, and are also reported to be the most likely to drop out of courses (Morris 1994). New courses tend to attract women who have recently moved to the area and who are not Welsh speaking (Garland 1994; Willox and Virgin 1992). As one training provider in Gwynedd reported:

21

> I do have some [Welsh speakers] but not as many as the English. They are quite successful when they come on the course and they enjoy it when they come here but they have the timidity which maybe the English people don't .... I think also the idea among the Welsh males [is] that the women should stay in the home. The husbands we have most trouble with are often the Welsh ones because they have got used to the traditional way of life where the woman has their meals on the table at a particular time ...
> (Willox and Virgin 1992, p. 31)

and an education provider in Gwynedd stated:

> Yes, I suppose that it is a lack of confidence in the sense that there has been a lack of experience there, most of them have been having children since they were twenty. They haven't had the work experience, no experience with interviews etc. Also there is sometimes a lack of confidence in doing things in English, and put the two together and it is quite profound ...
> (Willox and Virgin 1992, p. 30)

Morris's report shows an under-representation of Welsh speakers among the women mature students at University College of North Wales, Bangor, and University of Wales, Aberystwyth, both in strong Welsh-speaking areas. The same pattern was found in access courses among FE colleges in Gwynedd and Clwyd (Garland 1992; Morris 1994).

Ethnic minorities

The vast majority of over 16 year-olds in Wales described their ethnic group as white in the 1991 Census, the proportion from ethnic minorities ranging from 4.1 per cent in South Glamorgan to 1.2 per cent in Gwent and other areas (North West Regional Research Laboratory 1993). This figure consists largely of Indian, Pakistani, Bangladeshi, Caribbean, African, Chinese and Somali groups, together with many other smaller minority groups. Languages spoken include Gujerati, Bengali, Punjabi, Hindu, Urdu, Pushto, Vietnamese, Chinese (mainly Cantonese), Greek, Turkish and various other dialects.

Women from ethnic minorities constitute 1.1 per cent of women of working age in Wales, of whom just under half are economically active compared with nearly two-thirds of white women. There are variations between groups: Indian and Chinese women are more likely to be economically active, Pakistanis and Bangladeshis less so (Owen 1994).

Although there are dangers of making comparisons with such small numbers, nevertheless the authors of a report analysing 10 per cent 1991 Census data report that:

> Fewer whites than other groups possess educational qualifications – 11.9 per cent compared to 20.1 per cent. However, the TEC area with the largest proportion of other groups, South Glamorgan, has a different pattern. The white population has an above average proportion with qualifications (16.4 per cent) and the other groups a below average proportion (15.6 per cent).
> (North West Regional Research Laboratory 1993, p. 128)

There are many highly qualified women from ethnic minorities in Wales, but at the same time there are special training needs in South Glamorgan especially. South Glamorgan has a larger non-white population than other areas in Wales and one of the oldest established multi-cultural communities in Britain centred in the Cardiff Docks area, a community which has suffered high rates of unemployment. Cardiff has attracted many financial services industries through inward investment; it is also an administrative centre and has large educational and health establishments, accounting for the higher than average qualifications basis of the residents.

3.3   SCHOOLGIRLS' OCCUPATIONAL CHOICES

In 1988, the Cardiff Women's Training Roadshow, held over two days in University College Cardiff, attracted over 2,000 South Wales schoolgirls and numerous women to an exhibition of education, training and employment opportunities. It focused on areas that women traditionally have not entered. Some 70 Welsh role models (women who do jobs traditionally done by men, such as bank manager, airline pilot, taxidermist and engineers) were questioned by the visitors, and 50 careers officers held group discussions with the girls about their life and career plans. There were also exhibitions, videos and career games.

The event was evaluated with funding from the Welsh Office, and 500 of the girls were followed up six months later to ascertain whether they remembered visiting the Roadshow and, if so, whether it had had any impact on their option and career choices (see T. Rees 1992; Pilcher et al. 1988, 1989a, 1989b, 1990). The schoolgirls were asked if they could recall any of the role models at the Roadshow. They reconstructed in their memories the bank manager as a bank clerk, and the airline pilot as a stewardess. One of the role models was asked if she was 'really an engineer'. When she asked the girls why they doubted it, they explained it was because she 'had a hand bag' (T. Rees 1992).

The schoolgirls' option and career choices were highly gender stereotyped. Their views of the future were also informed by an anticipation of a 'broken' career to take care of children. They also expressed a strong desire to stay near their home: this restricted their education, training and career choices to those available in the locality. The combined effect is schoolgirls' unwillingness to invest in their human capital.

Moreover, the research revealed that the girls, in particular working-class South Wales Valleys girls with no expectations of gaining qualifications, felt that they had very little control over their future – your future was 'just something that happened to you' – the result of decisions made by others. Careers officers reported that, again especially in Valleys' communities, parental influences on career choices tended to steer the girls in a highly traditionally female direction. Educational achievement levels in Mid Glamorgan are the lowest in the country (see Chapter 4).

This leaves a legacy of underqualified women in Valley communities whose needs will require imaginative programmes. There are some examples of such innovative programmes (such as the Community University of the Valleys, the Dove workshop, and the Valleys Women's Roadshow – see Chapter 5) but they tend to be piecemeal, small-scale and insecurely funded.

Option choices in schools and participation in further and higher education remain firmly along gender-stereotypical lines as the next chapter demonstrates. In North Wales, there are a number of initiatives which seek to widen girls' choices. Clwyd County Council adopted *Genderwatch* monitoring schedules for schools. These were translated into Welsh and made available to all secondary schools in the county, with Equal Opportunities Commission funding. A postgraduate certificate of education course at University College of North Wales, Bangor, on equal opportunities has developed research projects among student teachers during their practical placements in local schools. This 'helps teacher-educators to keep in touch with progress in schools and thus to understand the problems facing student teachers' (Daniel 1994). Student teachers' own awareness of equal opportunities issues is heightened by participation in this project.

24

Research in North Wales has shown a clear trend in coupling arts subjects with the Welsh language and women teachers, and science teaching with the English language and male teachers. Such trends reinforce patterns of gender-specific option and career choices because of the lack of role models challenging the language/subject/gender pattern. Research into attitudes, aspirations and opportunities for Welsh-speaking sixth formers reveals that girls are more likely to study arts subjects through the medium of Welsh at 'A' level, and to remain in Wales to pursue higher education through the medium of the Welsh language. By contrast, boys are more likely to study science and technology through the medium of English (due to the lack of opportunities to study such subjects in the Welsh language) and to move away for higher education. As Daniel (1994) reports:

> One implication of this trend is that it is women teachers in Wales who are more likely to provide role models of close affiliation with the language, culture and geographical area, while male teachers will continue to reflect the wide experience and opportunities with which 'male' subjects and the English language are associated. Women are more likely anyway to consider teaching as a first career choice and to be able to go into Welsh medium teacher training. How might this influence the choices female pupils make in the future?

The fact that the position of the Welsh language as a core subject in the National Curriculum has recently been weakened removes the imperative to develop Welsh medium teacher training further. As a consequence, its association with gender-specific subject teaching is likely to continue.

This section (together with the statistical data in the next chapter) shows that occupational choices among schoolchildren in Wales remain highly gender specific. This has important implications for the future training needs of women. It also means that it is important to diversify the subjects that women teachers specialise in, especially women teaching through the medium of Welsh. Finally, it points to an urgent need for schoolgirls (and boys) to have earlier careers education and advice, before gender stereotypes become too rigid for alternative paths to be considered.

3.4   WOMEN EMPLOYEES

The most detailed British evidence study of employers' training policies (Training Agency 1989) suggests that they are less likely to sponsor women for training than men, and those that do sponsor women are more likely to do so for short courses. This is partly because in those professions and occupations whose occupants are more likely to be offered training, managers and technical staff are much more likely to be men. Unfortunately we do not have data at the level of Wales (although Welsh employers contributed to the British study) with which to make comparisons. However, we do know that there are proportionately fewer women in such posts, and research projects on South Wales suggest a broadly similar pattern (G. Rees and Fielder 1992; G. Rees et al. 1989, 1991). Chapter 4 gives statistical information on employees receiving job-related training.

Part of the WDA strategy for economic development for Wales has been to encourage inward investment of financial services and information technology companies. Certainly employment in these sectors has increased. In a study of 20 major employers' demand for information technology skills in South East Wales, most were in the process of changing their training arrangements as previous strategies had proved unsatisfactory, or as the numbers using new technologies had increased. Training in low-level technologies is in a state of flux (G. Rees et al. 1989, 1991).

Three training models were identified: in-house training, the 'cascade model' and external training. Large employers use different training strategies for different categories of staff. Most organise training for low-level IT skills in-house. For some this is part of a company induction course, for others there were formal training sessions over a matter of days or weeks, for others again it was a case of 'sitting with Nellie', depending on the complexity of the work. Companies in the financial services sector retrained staff to update their skills as more sophisticated systems were brought in. In one major bank, there is a training function within the word-processing unit which deals specifically with low-level skills. The courses are modular and usually run for one day, two at the most. More and more of the bank's training is done in-house now, as the need for it has increased due to the implementation of new systems, and it is now more cost-effective than external training.

In one major retailer where all the training is done in-house and on the job, 'very much a sitting-with-Nellie thing' (South Wales store training officer), departments are staffed above their required level in order to allow sufficient time and resources to accommodate the training.

Three employers reported using the 'cascade' model of training, that is training up a member of staff who is then responsible for training others. An advertising organisation's personnel officer reported that so far, the 'main secretaries from each department have been identified as the first to go on the

26

course. It is then hoped a certain amount of "cascade training" will take place within the departments'.

Employers in the study criticised the training provided by computer equipment suppliers. In some cases this is because such suppliers underestimate how much women staff already know:

> staff have reported that some of the training courses have been 'very slow'. For example, the secretarial staff already have a background knowledge of things such as how to format a disk, and have said there was really no need for them to attend the first course, but the training provider will not allow people to start on level 2 if they are not convinced the trainee has reached their standard on level 1. (Personnel officer, advertising business, South Glamorgan, quoted in G. Rees et al. 1989, p. 42)

The two studies revealed that for the most part, new information technologies in a range of industries in South Wales are organised in such a way that women's skills are not developed to their full potential. Rather, work organisation patterns separate out routine information technology requirements from more creative work. This has led to the deskilling of many women. Old gendered orders of work organisation are informing the design of workplaces. New technologies have the potential to allow women to develop their skills, as we can see in advanced technological companies in Germany, where women secretaries and women arts and social science graduates are being trained up to fill skill shortages in jobs where technological skills are required alongside other skills such as good communication, team-working and diagnostics skills (T. Rees 1994b).

In sectors which are major employers of women there are divergent trends in training policies. In the retail sector, a study of employers in the Bridgend area has showed that there are clear indications that some major chain stores, faced with shortages of school leavers, are training up existing women staff to take on supervisory and even management roles (G. Rees et al. 1989). The practice of contracting-out services such as catering and cleaning has led to different patterns of training women in Wales: while the cleaning industry has adopted a strategy of intensification, catering has moved toward improving employment conditions through, for example, enhanced training and promotion prospects (G. Rees and Fielder 1992).

Many of the professions which employ large numbers of women are developing opportunities for in-service training, given the drive towards credentialism, that is, the demand by a profession for more and more qualifications. The health service for example, a major employer of women in Wales, has invested considerably in training its staff. Similarly, in FE, many lecturers who started their careers as practitioners are now seeking qualifications for the job of teaching others which they have been doing for many years. An in-depth study of one such cohort described by Salisbury (1994) illustrated that the women returning to training felt many of the same anxieties about their capabilities as the mature age women students returning to study. Some of the women FE teachers had typically female 'accidental' career trajectories:

> I remember my first day as a teacher clearly, it's a funny story but I was actually a part-time secretary for the Vice-Principal of the College at the time. Well, a woman in Business Studies was taken ill – she died a few days later actually – and the Principal asked me to step in to help the Department out … so I was a typist one morning and a teacher the same afternoon … I was really thrown in at the 'deep end!'
> (Respondent quoted in Salisbury 1994, p. 147)

Although some women employees in Wales are benefiting from training opportunities in the drive to credentialise, this also serves to widen the gap between those with and without qualifications. As it is women who tend to take time off for domestic responsibilities and to work part-time in jobs where they are less likely to be offered training (and indeed promotion) possibilities, the low economic activity rates of women and high proportions of women working part-time in Wales are highly significant.

It should be remembered too that many women in Wales work part-time, or in other jobs where training is rarely offered to employees.

3.5   ECONOMICALLY INACTIVE AND UNEMPLOYED WOMEN

The ERES (1994) study of the economically inactive in Wales described earlier included a statistically representative sample of economically inactive men and women in the Principality. The findings showed that financial help in undertaking a course was very important for both men and women, and that for women aged between 16 and 34, and to a lesser extent the 25–34 year age group, it was considered important that courses be held in the morning: this is undoubtedly linked to the lack of childcare provision. Some 55 per cent of women (two-thirds of whom were aged 16–34) would welcome undertaking a course at home. All the females in the study emphasised how important it was that courses should be provided locally. Financial assistance for childcare was considered very important by 80 per cent of women aged between 16 and 34, while childcare at the place of training was considered important by 50 per cent of the women. Single-sex training was not considered important by men or women, but other research has showed that while this feature did not particularly attract women onto a course, it was appreciated during the training (see Essex et al. 1986; T. Rees 1992).

The measurement of unemployment among women is distorted by the eligibility criteria for claiming benefit, given that many older women are still paying the married women's reduced insurance stamp, some are not deemed 'available' for work because of domestic commitments although they would take a job if offered, and others have not acquired enough contributions because they have been working part-time, or are only seeking part-time employment and therefore do not count according to the criteria. Hence claimant statistics are not an accurate measure of unemployment among women. Many of the courses designed for women returners are attracting unemployed women, whether they are claimants or not.

A study in South Glamorgan discovered a hitherto hidden degree of unemployment among young men and women aged 16–18, the 'disappeared'. Up to one-fifth of young people of this age group, the study found, who are no longer eligible for unemployment benefit were not in employment, education or training – they had slipped through the net. Teenage mothers are one category of 'disappeared' young women with special needs, and a disproportionate number of the disappeared had been in care. The authors interviewed 26 such young people and concluded:

> Whilst we must avoid constructing stereotypes, almost all respondents recounted past experiences which might be viewed as a 'tangle of pathologies': non-school attendance; fractured childhoods as a result of 'broken homes'; at least temporary homelessness; brushes with the law; sexual and physical abuse and other forms of violence; and drug misuse.
> (Istance et al. 1994a, p. 5)

The 'disappeared' will be particularly difficult to attract back into education and training.

3.6   WOMEN RETURNERS

The high proportion of economically inactive women in Wales includes many who are considering returning to the labour force at some stage in the future (C. Rees and Willox 1991a, 1991b; Willox and Virgin 1992). Women returners are diverse in terms of their education, training and labour market experiences, but also tend to share many characteristics which traditionally education and training systems have been ill-equipped to accommodate. These include loss of confidence, combined with outdated substantive skills, domestic responsibilities and an inability to pay substantial fees and travel costs (see Essex et al. 1986; T. Rees 1992). Those initiatives which have responded best to these needs of women returners have tended to be organised by women themselves in the voluntary sector, such as the South Glamorgan Women's Workshop which enjoys European renown (see Chapter 5). More recently, however, traditional education and training providers have sought to recruit women returners, particularly as the numbers of young people taking up places have declined.

Studies of women returners in Wales (as elsewhere) show lack of confidence to be a crucial problem (Essex et al. 1986; Lodge et al. 1991; MacNamara 1990; New 1991; T. Rees 1992). Garland's (1994) study of female mature students returning to learn in a higher education setting in North Wales portrays their lack of confidence and feelings of guilt about neglecting family responsibilities, together with tensions experienced when partners find it difficult to accommodate the way in which education has changed their lives. Severe problems of time management are common to such students (Lodge et al. 1991).

The women-only aspect of training is much appreciated by trainees who experience it. Similarly, trainees report the importance of having women tutors when learning new technologies. As trainees at the South Glamorgan Women's Workshop reported to MacNamara (1990, p. 48):

> I was going through a divorce at the time and would cry at the most strange times.
> I only got through it because of the other women's support. It was my 'island',
> a place where I could be myself, believe in my abilities.

> I was frightened of the computers but no-one put me down, a woman tutor gave
> me support, she didn't laugh.

> I didn't feel daft, asking a woman tutor what bit of wire went where.

> I couldn't have coped with a male tutor. I would have felt intimidated.

Courses for women returners tend to target those with few or no qualifications and train them in basic level skills. Some are then successful in gaining employment. However, in order to take advance level training, they need to acquire prerequisite qualifications to satisfy matriculation requirements. Given the highly tiered nature of much of the Welsh labour market, there is an urgent need for routes of progression for women returners to be set up within the education and training systems. These should run alongside guidance and counselling to prevent women taking up posts below their potential from which there are no opportunities for training or promotion.

3.7   WOMEN IN BUSINESS

Self-employment is an important dimension of the Welsh economy especially in rural areas. The number of women who participate in their partner's business remains unknown. However, a recent European Union directive which seeks to ensure that farmers' wives are eligible for pensions and sick leave should be beneficial to many farmers' wives' in Wales who are in effect business partners, but who do not appear in the figures (see Ashton 1994). Self-employment and small businesses as potential sources of employment creation are particularly important to those parts of Wales which are unlikely to be attractive to inward investors because of their physical remoteness.

In Wales, 92 per cent of white women in work are employees, while 8 per cent are self-employed (a higher figure than in either England or Scotland). Self-employment is twice as high as this among women from ethnic minorities: even though they constitute 800 out of the 38,600 self-employed women in Wales. Self-employment is highest among only Pakistani (36.1 per cent) and Chinese (32.7 per cent) women, and lowest among women from other Asian ethnic groups (Owen 1994).

The EC-funded Athena project was initiated by Gateway Europe, the European Commission's University Enterprise Training Partnership based in Wales. It arose out of the EC Task Force Human Resources, Education, Training and Youth *Skills Development Project* which examined skills needs in 26 regions of the European Union. The Athena project was a partnership of teams in six European regions which sought to explore the issue of women and skill shortages. The focus of each team's work was determined by the particular needs of the region concerned: the focus in Wales was on the training needs of women setting up in business (Gateway Europe 1993a). A system of 'braiding' between the teams allowed the cross-fertilisation of ideas through visits and exchanges. A synthesis report records the findings of the Athena project (Gateway Europe 1993b) and recommendations on women and training derived from a dissemination conference held in North Wales in spring 1994 have been brought out in a follow-up report (T. Rees 1994c).

The Welsh team within the Athena project focused on women and enterprise because of the importance of self-employment and small businesses to the regional economy, in particular rural areas where one in four jobs is accounted for by self-employment. The project consisted of the collection of labour-market data and a series of interviews with key business and support agencies. A survey of women entrepreneurs was carried out with some follow-up interviews.

The research revealed that there are three main types of women entrepreneurs. These were termed 'sole employee', 'budding entrepreneurs' and 'enterprising woman'. Each type had different training and support needs. A 'sole employee' has no ambition to expand her business and is strongly attracted to the way of life because of the flexibility it affords. The 'budding entrepreneur' may be involved in the business with others, such as a partner with whom she may or may not have a personal relationship. She is likely to want to expand the business and is willing to delegate tasks. The 'enterprising woman' has probably been in business for more than five years and already employs 20 people or more. She may have a variety of goals such as expansion, diversification, or simply survival. Women in business, then, have a variety of needs.

Business training was identified as one of a number of key issues by the women in the survey. Mainstream training available for people seeking to set up or expand their businesses was deemed unsuitable by many women because of the hours, style of delivery, lack of childcare facilities and so on. Pre-training is rarely available, to develop confidence, help develop a feasible business plan, and to encourage women to realise that such skills that they do have are relevant to running a business. In Australia, such pre-training skills include 'the naming of parts', in which women who have been managing household budgets on a low income are shown how this is the same as managing cash flow in a business. The demystifying of jargon through training in itself can help to increase confidence (T. Rees 1992).

There were no examples of courses found in Wales available for male partners of women wanting to set up in business, although such courses exist in Denmark. Given that so many small businesses are in effect family concerns, as either partnerships or one of the parties acting in a support role, then training provision ought to accommodate this. Training needs audits for small businesses are the responsibility of the TECs, but the Athena project reported that they should be encouraged to 'identify the special training needs of women in business and provide appropriate services for women to expand and develop their businesses' (Gateway Europe 1993a, p. 5).

Training rarely accommodates the fact that it is families who want to set up in business: training is geared towards the individual. Research in rural Wales showed women just as likely to enrol on business development courses as men, but often with different purposes and needs (Gateway Europe 1993a). The most recent initiative from Chwarae Teg is a systematic survey of business support services in Wales to identify any specific gender measures, including training initiatives, which support women setting up and running their own businesses. A report is being published to outline actions these agencies can take to improve services to women entrepreneurs in the future. This initiative is being funded by the Welsh Office and is due to be completed in late 1994.

There have been a number of developments in the field of business training in Wales. The Wales Co-operative Centre, set up by the Wales Trades Union Congress with European and local authority funding, runs training courses for 'enterprise trainers' to assist groups of people wanting to set up co-operatives in Wales. Women have participated in the courses and some of the co-ops to be set up have been all-women teams. These include Bargoed Blouses, one of the first to be set up. However, there are no special measures to assist women, and gender monitoring of participants of courses does not take place systematically.

This section shows that on the whole, business support training tends to be gender blind and does not accommodate the needs of members of family businesses, or women (Allen and Truman 1993; Gateway Europe 1993a; T. Rees 1992). Childcare needs, hours of delivery, and confidence-building as well as the more usual training, should all be taken into account.

3.8   CONCLUSION

Research on women and training in Wales is patchy: some groups of women, some parts of Wales and some parts of the system are much better documented than others. There is very little research available on the needs and experiences of ethnic minority women in Wales, nor systematic work on provision in the Welsh language. Some areas appear to be hardly documented at all, for example the potential for new developments in distance learning for a largely rural area. The extent to which women employees are trained is not researched comprehensively, and yet the development of job-

33

related training for women is vital to the economic success of their employers. The needs of unemployed women are particularly difficult to gauge.

Nevertheless some findings emerge which point to the success of training which is tailor-made for women, and the difficulties some women have in taking advantage of education and training opportunities on offer because of childcare commitments, costs, travel difficulties, confidence problems or lack of prerequisite qualifications. There is a clear need to mainstream some of the lessons from examples of best practice (that is, have them adopted by other training providers): to an extent this is already being done in some FE colleges.

The lack of women in top jobs revealed by research in a political arithmetic exercise produced results that shocked many in Wales. More thorough-going research is now needed on the barriers women employees face when seeking job-related training and promotion.

Routes of progression in training are needed for women returners; much provision directed at them leads them straight into jobs in the workplace below their potential. Lifelong careers guidance and counselling for all are now needed. This is increasingly recognised as important in many of the other EU Member States, given the dynamism of the labour market, the impact of new technologies and the increasingly short shelf life of many skills and occupations. More research on the *effectiveness* of education and training for women would be helpful, through a follow-up or 'tracking' study of women on a variety of courses, particularly those for returners.

The prevalence of women among part-time workers and their tendency to be excluded from continuing training is a particular problem in Wales. Training for new technologies has so far failed to help women to reach their potential in Wales because of gendered patterns of work organisation.

Research has shown that young women, especially teenage mothers and others not participating in education, training or employment, are a cause for concern, given the widening gap between their marketability and that of employees in an increasingly credentialised workplace. Careers education and advice need to begin earlier in schools, and strenuous efforts need to be made to encourage girls to appreciate that they are likely to be in the workforce for most of their adult lives, and hence their education, training and career 'choices' are important. The case has to be put across firmly that it is worth their while, and that of others, to invest in their skills.

34

Self-employment and small businesses are vital to the Welsh economy and the Athena project has proved useful in identifying women entrepreneurs' needs: these are now beginning to be addressed through Chwarae Teg. More work is to be done in training women in both substantive and business skills to enable them to engage in the labour market on their own terms.

In conclusion, the evidence from the research literature gives some clear indications of how post-compulsory education and training in Wales goes some way towards meeting the needs of women and the need for women's skills, but there is still a considerable waste of talent and under-development of women's skills. Further research would be helpful in shedding light on some key issues identified here, but it is already clear that mainstreaming good practice would be highly effective. The next chapter explores what can be learnt from statistical sources.

4.   PATTERNS AND RECENT TRENDS: A REVIEW OF STATISTICS

4.1   INTRODUCTION

This chapter reports the main quantitative, statistical evidence concerning the situation of women in education and training in Wales. In this, we draw on data gathered by different agencies, much of which is generated from official sources, to provide summary data across Wales as a whole (Welsh Office, Careers Service in Wales, Universities Statistical Record, etc.). In fact, a substantial body of evidence on the situation of women in education and training is currently available in published form even though, as was necessary here, it often calls for a major re-calculation exercise in order for the gender dimension to emerge clearly. The need to complement this with unpublished material should not obscure the value of this existing published documentation. Some of the main tables are presented in the text itself; others are contained in Appendix III (and indicated with the prefix 'A').

4.2   THE POSITION OF WOMEN IN EDUCATION AND TRAINING IN BRITAIN: AN OFFICIAL SUMMARY

Our study is focused specifically on Wales and cannot give comprehensive comparisons with other parts of Britain. (Other such reviews of the situation in Britain as a whole includes a study within the EOC's own Research Discussion Series, such as Clarke 1991.) Nevertheless, where regional comparisons are readily available, they reveal the scale of problems faced in Wales, both in general and for women in particular. It is also useful to consider as our starting point the overall context of Britain; this sets the scene for our main analysis of Wales.

That context can be established by reference to a recent official summary of the position of women in post-school education compiled by the Department for Education (1993). The summary section of the bulletin (pp.1–2) reads:

(i)   Girls generally achieved better GCSE results than boys.

(ii)   Women were more likely to participate in education at ages 16 and 17 than men. Men were more likely to be in part-time education among these age groups.

(iii)   Women were more likely to take and pass 'A' levels than men. However, male candidates had a slightly better success rate.

(iv)   Women undergraduates were more likely to study arts and humanities (including business and teacher training) and less likely to study sciences than men.

(v)   The unemployment rate among female graduates was much lower than among their male counterparts. The types of work which graduates entered also differed considerably between the sexes.

(vi)   In the population as a whole men generally had a higher level of qualification than women. However the gap is much narrower among the younger age groups.

(vii)   There were more women teachers than men. Women were particularly numerous among primary teachers. The proportion of women was highest among younger teachers.

(viii) Women aged 18 or over were more likely to be participating in education than men. This was particularly true among older age groups.

(ix)   Women were more likely to be studying on shorter further education courses than men. They obtained more vocational qualifications than men but men gained more at higher levels.

It is a useful introduction because it shows that the patterns and dynamics at play are now more complex than in earlier decades when women were consistently disadvantaged on almost all indicators of educational attainment and participation. It also suggests the value of a detailed examination of the evidence, as the summary headlines can hide other aspects and also wide variations concerning the specific difficulties confronted by both women and men in education and training. That summary tends to minimise the extent of the barriers and bottlenecks that still exist for too many women in their access to and experience of education and training, and in having these recognised and translated in the labour market. This is of particular relevance for this study.

The Welsh data confirm that major strides have been made; there are also deep-rooted inequalities yet to be overcome.

4.3   THE SITUATION IN WALES

Education and training for 16–18 year-olds

School attainments – too many without any qualifications in Wales

Whilst this particular study is predominantly about the situation post-school, the natural starting point for such a review is consideration of the basis of educational attainment acquired during schooling. This shows that girls and young women have caught up with or surpassed their male

37

classmates in levels of qualification in Wales, as in the rest of the UK (recognising the important issues of subject choice that persist), as is described above and shown in detail in Table 4.1.

What is particularly striking from the regional comparisons in Table 4.1, however, is the disadvantage suffered by Welsh students, female and male, in the relatively high proportions of school-leavers with no graded qualification of even the most basic sort, while attainment of at least two 'A' levels – the normal passport to higher education – is comparatively low.

Table 4.1   Percentages of all school-leavers with 2 or more 'A' levels (3 or more Highers in Scotland) and with no graded results in school qualifications,[1] by UK region and gender, 1990/91

UK region	Males		Females	
	A levels 2+	No graded results	A levels 2+[2]	No graded results
North	15.2	11.6	16.6	6.4
Yorkshire and Humberside	16.9	9.5	19.3	7.5
East Midlands	20.0	6.5	21.6	4.0
East Anglia	20.1	6.6	23.2	6.0
South East	24.4	8.3	26.5	5.4
– London	21.3	11.8	23.5	8.0
– Rest of SE	26.0	6.9	27.9	4.0
South West	23.4	4.8	22.2	4.0
West Midlands	19.0	7.4	21.4	5.2
North West	20.1	9.9	20.2	8.1
England	21.1	8.2	22.5	5.8
Scotland	23.9	11.7	29.2	8.9
Northern Ireland	24.8	16.1	31.3	9.8
WALES	16.9	16.0	21.9	10.3
UK TOTAL	21.3	9.2	23.5	6.5

Notes: [1] GCSE, CSE, SCE, 'A' or 'AS' levels or Highers, but not other vocational qualifications.
            [2] 3 or more Highers in Scotland.

Source: Central Statistical Office 1993, Table 5.7.

Unqualified female school-leavers are found in greater concentrations in Wales than in any of the other regions. Only in Wales does the percentage reach double figures. The slippage in the female share attaining at least two 'A' levels has not been as marked as with males (it is 'slippage' for, in the earlier post-war period, Wales was noted for its favourable rates of university preparation, as described in G. Rees and T. Rees 1980). The Welsh level is still well below the UK average for young women, however (21.9 per cent and 23.5 per cent respectively). This regional analysis for 1990/91 shows that for males, the proportion in Wales with no results is significantly greater than in all other parts of Great Britain (it is similar in Northern Ireland), and in only one region – the North of England – is there a lower percentage of leavers qualified with two or more 'A' levels.

Behind these main patterns there are substantial variations from one county to another in Wales on these dimensions of education and training. Table 4.2 gives the detail of the intra-Wales percentages of school-leavers with no school qualifications or graded results at all.

Table 4.2   Percentage of school-leavers in Wales who fail to achieve any graded result in school examinations,[1] by county and gender, 1991/92

County	Males	Females	Total
Clywd	11.4	9.0	10.2
Dyfed	11.2	7.0	9.2
Gwent	14.3	11.6	13.0
Gwynedd	11.7	6.3	9.1
Mid Glamorgan	22.4	15.4	19.0
Powys	8.1	3.2	5.7
South Glamorgan	16.5	12.1	14.3
West Glamorgan	12.1	11.5	11.8
Independents	6.3	1.2	4.2
WALES	14.2	10.4	12.4

Note: [1] GCSE, CSE, SCE, 'A' or 'AS' levels or Highers, but not vocational qualifications.
Source: Welsh Office 1994b, Table 9.10.

For both boys and girls, Mid Glamorgan exhibits the most apparent concentration of under-qualification. Nearly one in five of all school-leavers in this county – the most heavily populated in Wales – achieve no school qualification at all.

In summary,

> Welsh school-leavers do badly compared with leavers in other parts of Britain comparing both an indicator of success (proportion attaining at least two 'A' levels) and lack of success (those leaving with no graded result at all). While girls do better on the whole than boys, a higher proportion of girls leave school with no results than in any other region or country of the UK.

Immediate leaving or staying-on in education

When the focus turns to those who stay or leave education at the minimum age (Table 4.3), similar broad patterns are reproduced. This includes the higher participation by females than males. Across the counties of Wales, the lowest leaving rate for boys (Dyfed at 29.4 per cent) is higher than the highest for girls (28.6 per cent in Mid Glamorgan). But there is no close correlation between the ordering of counties in terms of lack of qualification and rates of early leaving – South Glamorgan, for instance, has one of the lowest rates of quitting education at age 16, but one of the highest rates of non-qualification. For young women in this regard, as opposed to young men, Mid Glamorgan is not so distinct: in this case, Clywd and Gwent show similar proportions quitting education.

Table 4.3   Percentages of 16 year-olds in Wales who (a) leave, (b) stay in education at minimum school leaving age, by county and gender, 1993

County	Males		Females		Total	
	a %	b %	a %	b %	a %	b %
Clywd	37.6	62.4	28.3	71.7	33.1	66.9
Dyfed	29.4	70.6	16.7	83.3	23.1	76.9
Gwent	36.3	63.7	28.5	71.5	32.5	67.5
Gwynedd	32.7	67.3	22.6	77.4	27.9	72.1
Mid Glamorgan	40.7	59.3	28.6	71.4	34.7	65.3
Powys	31.5	68.5	19.0	81.0	25.4	74.6
South Glamorgan	30.1	69.9	23.3	76.7	26.7	73.3
West Glamorgan	36.6	63.4	26.0	74.0	31.6	68.4
WALES	35.2	64.8	25.1	74.9	30.3	69.7

Source: Careers Service in Wales 1994, p. 3.

The main divide here is a rural/urban one: the proportion of young women staying on – in excess of 80 per cent in the rural counties of Dyfed and Powys, with a high figure in Gwynedd as well – contrasts with levels barely above 70 per cent in Clywd, Gwent, and Mid Glamorgan. The gap in the female rates between one county of Wales and another is in fact as large or larger than that between males and females. The figures also show that there is no simple correlation between youth labour market opportunities and staying on or leaving (what might be described, in labour market economics terms, as a 'discouraged student' and 'discouraged worker' effect). There may be a dearth of jobs in the rural areas but, even in the industrial counties where the staying-on rates are lowest, the youth labour market that might 'pull' young people out of school or college with the temptation of a wage, is scarcely flourishing. Indeed, these counties of Gwent, Clywd and Mid Glamorgan experience some of the worst youth labour market problems.

Since 1989, when pupil destination data have been regularly compiled by the Careers Services, they show just how rapid has been the increase in the rates of staying on (in this case tending to confirm the 'discouraged worker' thesis, as teenage employment opportunities have become dire over this period). In 1989, the female and male proportions still staying on in the autumn after passing 16 years were approximately 60 per cent and 45 per cent, respectively. By 1993, the same pattern is in evidence, albeit modified to the extent that the rate of increase of young men in post-16 participation from their lower starting point has been greater than for women (Table A1). The 1993 figures are 74.9 per cent (women) and 64.8 per cent (men). The gender gap has narrowed to 10 percentage points from the 15 point difference at the end of the 1980s. Nevertheless, women are on average still well ahead.

Other recent Careers Service figures reveal how the positive trend for young women and men towards larger numbers staying on in education at age 16 has another side (Careers Services in Wales 1994, p. 12). Very many have completed short courses or have dropped out of education by the age of 18, so that the 1993 age 16 level of 70 per cent falls to 40 per cent for 18 year-olds (two-thirds of the six in ten who had earlier stayed on in education in 1991). There is a methodological point to underline here: the immediate 16 year-old destination figures do not supply a basis on which to assess general participation in education 16–18. Other studies have described the large extent of flux occurring over this age period (see Istance et al. 1994).

The revealing aspect as regards gender is that *among those who stay on in education at age 16* the patterns among females and males are much more similar than among the entire cohort. Of those who decided to stay on in education in 1991, approximately two-thirds are still in education at age 18, which divides very evenly between 67.6 per cent women and 66.2 per cent men. The largest gap is seen between them in the initial decision to continue with formal education in some form and with the other routes and destinations at this age (see Table A1), not in the proportions who then continue studies once embarked.

In summary,

> There has been a very rapid increase in staying-on over the past five years – up from about half of 16 year-olds in 1989 to 70 per cent in 1993. Women stay on in education in significantly greater numbers than men of the same age, though the gap in this regard is narrower than five years ago. The staying-on rate for

women is highest in the rural counties of Wales. There is far less gender difference in retention among those who originally stayed on in education by the time they reach 18; approximately two-thirds of both men and women are still there at this age.

Youth training and the dismal job market

Concerning participation in the Youth Training programme (YT) – the main training available for those who do not continue in mainstream education or move into employment – fewer men and women altogether now move on to a place on YT at age 16 than they used to; overall numbers in Wales among the immediate school-leavers are down from over 9,000 in 1989 to less than 4,000 in 1993 (Table A1). Two-thirds of these were men in 1993 and the gender disparity is becoming more apparent over time (31.7 per cent female in that year compared with 39 per cent at the end of the 1980s). 15.5 per cent of the males of this age were in YT in the autumn after an early departure from school in 1993, the comparable female rate being only 7.6 per cent. Comparing all YT starts in Wales in 1992/93 – which include some 16 year-olds starting later than those described above, as well as some 17 and 18 year-olds starting or restarting in training, only 37 per cent of these were women (data supplied by the Welsh Office). Given that the value and standing of Youth Training is widely recognised as problematic, lower participation does not in itself indicate a female disadvantage.

One of the most worrying aspects of the figures reproduced in Table A1 is the collapse of the job market for the youngest adults leaving school at 16, many of them poorly qualified. As recently as the end of the 1980s, when there were many more 16 year-olds in Wales (37,898) than in 1993, 12 per cent left school to go into a job. By 1993, this percentage had halved, a fall still more dramatic given that the 6 per cent was of a significantly smaller age group (31,638). Seven per cent of the men found immediate employment compared with only 5.6 per cent of the women.

Despite the fact that there are many fewer jobs for the school-leaver, this has not resulted in a more substantial proportion of them having in-built training. Indeed, the majority of the jobs that are available are without in-built training: in 1993, two-thirds of them did not incorporate a planned training element, the same proportion as in 1989. Because of the overall drop in numbers of 16 year-olds, combined with the marked decline in the percentages going into a job at all, the numbers of this age going into a job *with* a planned training component immediately on leaving school has slumped badly in Wales. They fell from 1,687 to 683 (autumn for each year) – barely 40 per cent of the 1989 figure. All do badly, therefore, and women fare as badly as men: only 2.5 per cent of the entire male 16 year-old cohort went into a job *with* training in Wales in 1993, as did a mere 1.8 per cent of women.

The same data show that the proportion of the 16 year-olds in Wales who are either known to be without a job or training place or else are already missing from contact with the authorities (neither enrolling in school or college nor registering with the local Careers Office), and who are hence not entitled to Income Support or any other social benefits, has also gone up since 1989 – from 10 per cent to 12 per cent in 1993. It was higher still in 1991 at 16 per cent. This most recent downward trend over the 1990s gives little grounds for celebration; recent Cardiff University research has revealed the large numbers of 16 and 17 year-olds who remain 'missing' once the initial contact with the authorities has been lost, or who become jobless, or who themselves go 'missing' after a short period in training (Istance et al. 1994). Official statistics tell us little or nothing about these youngsters. Joblessness based on these estimates is several times in excess of the official indicator of need which is the numbers in the queue for a Youth Training place – the so-called 'Youth Guarantee Group'.

These young adults are among the most disadvantaged and marginal of their generation. And whereas much of the publicity that this group does attract is focused on those involved in crime, who are largely male, there are actually similar proportions of women and men who are already jobless or 'missing' from the education, training, and employment nets at the age of 16. The pupil destination snapshot reveals this to stand at 12.7 per cent of males and 11.9 per cent of females (Table A1). The greater aggregate female advantage in terms of educational participation does not, therefore, translate into an advantage across the board. Among the low achievers, who are increasingly marginal to mainstream structures and opportunities, young women and men are found in equal numbers.

In summary,

> For those at age 16 who do not stay in school or college, there is a declining proportion entering YT and, of these, the male majority is becoming more pronounced. As YT is widely recognised as problematic and of low status, of itself this should not be interpreted as evidence of female disadvantage (though participation in YT is certainly preferable to joblessness). The job market for

young people has collapsed, with fewer jobs available and a sharply declining number that incorporate a planned training element. Even fewer women enter a job with a training component at this age than men. Despite the apparent female advantage in terms of continued education, similar numbers of men and women now find themselves in the marginal situation of being out of education, training or employment.

Further and higher education

Further education: more women in open and evening programmes; more men in work-integrated programmes

Women now comprise the majority among the enrolments and students in further education (FE) in Wales. By November 1992 this numerical advantage had attained 54.5 per cent of Welsh FE enrolments (Table A3). This was up slightly from female percentages of approximately 51 per cent at the end of the 1980s. Over this period there has been a general expansion, just as there has in upper school and higher education student numbers. The 70,000 1987/88 figure had increased by nearly 20,000 over the next five years to stand at 89,688 by 1992/93.

There are important differences, however, in the patterns in mode of attendance between men and women. Women FE students represent a small majority of those studying full-time (53.6 per cent of the full-time enrolments which is close to the overall female proportion). Much more distinctly, many of these female students were in evening, open and distance learning courses (41.6 per cent of all women FE student enrolments) as compared with just under three in ten (29.2 per cent) of the male FE students. This reflects and parallels the situation in Access courses (see below). In all, nearly two-thirds of those studying in the evening, or in open or distance learning are women – 32,229 students or 63 per cent of all studying in these less traditional arrangements.

It is in those courses that are much more closely integrated to employment – sandwich and day and block release programmes – where men are better represented. They predominate among sandwich students (83 per cent) and make up approximately two-thirds of the day and block release students (66.5 per cent). In contrast, among those part-time day students who are not 'released' the balance is reversed (66/34 women to men). In other words, men easily outnumber women in those education and training courses in FE that combine periods of work experience with periods of more theoretical college-based study.

The same table (A3) shows, however, that with the continuation of the recession, employers have become increasingly reluctant to enter into these kinds of training arrangements linking FE with jobs, so that this traditional male advantage has recently been pared back. Whereas nearly 46 per cent of male FE enrolments were part-time day in 1987/88 – the large majority of these on day or block release – this had fallen to a third by November 1992. In all, over half the male FE enrolments at that earlier 1980s reference point were in sandwich or part-time day schedules, but the proportion was down to 36 per cent in the more recent year. Absolute as well as relative numbers underline the trends. Total sandwich course enrolments fell from 2,087 in 1987 to less than a thousand in 1992 (991). Block and day release students are down, despite the overall increase in FE numbers of 20,000 between these years, from 18,539 to 15,604. At the same time, part-time day students not 'released' rose in the interim: from a little over 6,000 to 10,000.

Evidence relating to qualifications being sought in FE confirm the patterns described above (Table A4). More women are found in the academic programmes leading to qualifications which otherwise can be acquired in schools, such as 'A' levels or GCSEs. About two-thirds of the GCSE course enrolments are women, and six in ten of the 'A' and 'AS' enrolments. On the other hand, many more men than women enrol in the technical programmes such the vocational BTEC certificate, diploma, and City and Guilds (and other regional examining body) routes. This is especially marked among the certificate-level and City and Guilds enrolments at approximately seven in ten men in both. This tendency is reversed for what are described as 'professional' qualifications aiming primarily at 'female' occupations: over 80 per cent of these enrolments, representing over a fifth of all female FE student enrolments, are women. (Only 5.6 per cent of the male enrolments at this level are found in these programmes.) There is a large minority of students in a residual group classified as 'unspecified qualifications'; these now account for nearly 20,000 of the 95,934 enrolments. Over six in ten of these are women.

Without exaggerating the extent of female disadvantage in FE – for women are now the majority of these students; the professional qualifications route is an important aspect of women's vocational preparation; and many women choose to pursue academic studies in these colleges – women are still well under-represented in the technical branches. And more are in courses that do not lead to any specified qualification at all.

45

In summary,

> In FE the picture is mixed as regards the position of women. They now make up a clear majority of the students and trainees catered for by this sector, and many attend in the evening or through open or distance learning. Yet a third of the male FE students in Wales are in part-time day programmes as opposed to a quarter of the women, and two-thirds of the 'released' students are men – more men occupy those places most closely integrated to employment. In general, though, these openings are drying up. Female students outnumber the men in the 'academic' courses while men are more numerous in pursuit of the BTEC and City and Guilds technical qualifications. Not all of these offer 'marketable' routes to jobs, but some do. More women are found in the courses not leading to any specified qualification at the end of it.

Non-university higher education

Student numbers in the non-university higher education sector grew substantially as well over the past five years or so (Table A6). Catering for approximately 20,000 students in 1987/88, the figure now stands at 33,000. Of these, 47 per cent are women – approaching the female share of the age group (48–49 per cent). This is well up from the 41/59 balance in evidence in 1987/88. More women than men are enrolled full-time, both as a proportion of full-time students (53.5 per cent) and as the share of female students in non-university HE. Nearly 61 per cent of the women in this sector are on conventional full-time schedules, whereas less than half the men are (47 per cent). Much of the growth of student numbers in this sector can be accounted for by those studying on a full-time basis, growing from approximately 9,000 in 1987 to well over 17,000 by 1992. Taking these trends together, it is not surprising that the ratio of female to male full-time equivalent students now approaches equality (47.7 per cent women in 1991/92, compared with 43.4 per cent in 1987/88) (Table A2).

But, as in FE, more men are part-time day students, especially those on some form of release linked to employment. Two-thirds of the sandwich students, integrating study and employment in a long-cycle course, are men. And this form of programme has not diminished in the same way as in FE; it accounts for 17 per cent of the male non-university HE students and has grown from 3,402 enrolments in 1987 to 4,582 in 1992. Nor has day and block release fallen as in FE – numbers in this case growing from 5,200 in 1987 to nearly 7,500 in the most recent year. Men make up the majority of the day and block release students, but the share is falling and it now divides 60/40 compared with two-thirds/one-third at the end of the 1980s. Unlike FE, the evening, open and distance route is not so significant, nor is it growing over time.

While the patterns and trends surveyed suggest that non-university HE institutions are more equal than the FE colleges, data on enrolments in different subjects of study reveal some familiar patterns (Table A6). Adopting a difference of 75/25 or more as an indicator of continued wide imbalance, this is in evidence in six of the 16 subject lines. Three of these are 'female' programmes: education (75.6 per cent), 'other medical' (79.5 per cent), and the tiny languages line (82.1 per cent). The three 'male' lines of study are mathematics and computing (79.9 per cent), architecture etc. (89.5 per cent), and – inevitably – the engineering and technology programme which is still primarily a male preserve (93.8 per cent of the students). There are, however, examples of large programmes where men and women are much more evenly represented. This is the case in the largest programme in non-university HE – business and administration – and a similar equality of numbers is found in another popular subject area, creative arts and design.

This is a sector that is easy to overlook in comparison with the more famous university institutions. Yet it is an important one, providing high-level programmes often in vocational fields. Many of the students, especially the men, do not fit a traditional full-time 'model' of the student, accounting for nearly half of the male students in non-university HE. But the number of full-time students is growing, and many women choose this route, as a process of 'academic drift' reinforced by funding formulae pull these institutions to conform increasingly to the models offered by the university sector.

In summary,

> The non-university HE sector has grown significantly over recent years, as has the share of women among its students. As in FE, more women are studying full-time (53.5 per cent) while men are the majority in programmes directly linked to employment, such as sandwich or release courses. Enrolments in these latter courses have grown over recent years, in contrast to the situation in FE, and the male advantage in them is being reduced over time. Despite relative evenness of enrolments in some subjects, others remain sharply divided into 'male' and 'female' lines, especially mathematics and computing, architecture and building, and engineering and technology for men, and education and medically related courses for women.

University undergraduates: equality of numbers, some subjects still markedly divided

Enrolments among Welsh undergraduates in the different subject areas throughout UK universities (Table A9) display many of the same features as in non-university HE. Overall numbers of female students have grown to such a degree that they now are a slight majority (50.6 per cent). But the experience of a university undergraduate education is a different one for many women and men. The three most popular subjects for women out of the ten lines altogether in the table, which account for over six in ten of female undergraduates, are medicine and health (22 per cent); administration, business, and social studies (20.3 per cent); and languages, literature, etc. (18.8 per cent). The three corresponding popular programmes for men account for an even higher proportion (63.2 per cent of all male undergraduates) and, as for women, administration, business and social studies figures prominently (19.5 per cent). The other two popular programmes are, however, in the sciences which still remain male preserves. A quarter of Welsh undergraduate men in UK universities are in the biological and physical sciences, and nearly a fifth (18.7 per cent) are in faculties of engineering and technology.

Adopting the same demanding criterion of gender *imbalance* in subject areas as in the previous section (three-quarters/one quarter or more), three of the ten subjects are markedly unequal in these terms. The 'female' subjects are education (82.7 per cent) and languages, literature and area studies (76.8 per cent), while the 'male' subject area, unsurprisingly, is engineering and technology (88.3 per cent). Of course, this sort of comparison is heavily dependent on the level of aggregation adopted in the subject classification; a finer set of course distinctions would doubtless reveal a greater number of subjects with uneven patterns of recruitment.

If instead a minimum 60/40 balance is taken as indicative of relative *equality* of numbers, such evenness of recruitment is not unusual for it is found in another four of the ten subject areas. These, with female percentages noted, are in: agriculture, forestry, and veterinary science (41.5 per cent); administration, business, and social studies (51.7 per cent); arts other than languages (52.8 per cent); and multidisciplinary courses (56.4 per cent).

These results might be expected to be found anywhere in the UK, and are not specific to Wales in the main patterns they reveal. The statistics in Table A10 give an indication, however, of the extent to which Welsh women are enrolled in the same as, or different, proportions from female UK undergraduates overall, and Welsh male undergraduates in relation to the UK male averages. They give an indicator, in other words, of the specificity of the Welsh patterns of enrolment set against the benchmark averages of Welsh undergraduates to all undergraduates in the UK, with males and female rates calculated separately. (In this case, therefore, they are not at all affected by male/female differences of subject enrolments.)

The table indicates both the direction and scale of the departures from the main averages. The '+' signs in Table A10 show a comparative over-representation of Welsh women in medicine and health, architecture and other related studies, languages and literature, and in other arts. The under-representation is in education; engineering and technology; biological and physical sciences; administration, business, and social science; and in the multidisciplinary field. In three of the examples of under-representation, the difference is as great as a fifth, and included in these three is the subject area of engineering and technology. In other words, women are not only seriously absent from advanced technological studies, but Welsh women are even further behind the averages for female shares in these faculties in the UK taken as a whole. (They are also under-represented in the other scientific subjects of agriculture, forestry and veterinary science, and of biological and physical science.)

Without exaggerating the importance of all the science fields or denigrating the subject areas which women choose to study, it is notable that it is in the sciences where Welsh women are under-represented, not only and obviously in relation to men, *but in relation to female undergraduates in the rest of the UK as well.*

In summary,

> Welsh women undergraduates now slightly outnumber Welsh males studying at first degree level in UK universities. Apart from large numbers of both men and women in business, administration, and social studies courses, the most common subjects for each are not the same – many women study education and medically-related fields while large numbers of men are attracted to the sciences. Lack of women in science courses and especially in engineering and technology thus remain hurdles still to be overcome. In several other subject areas relative equality of numbers is beginning to be attained. Of particular concern, however, is that Welsh women are under-represented in the science fields not only in relation to men but in relation to other British female students as well.

Similar patterns for postgraduates

Even at the postgraduate level in universities, an advanced level of study where female recruitment for long lagged well behind, overall numbers are becoming ever more equal (Table A11). By the end of 1992, the balance of Welsh female to male postgraduates stood at 44/56. As with undergraduates, many of the students at this level are accounted for in a small number of popular postgraduate courses/subjects, with relatively few spread across the remaining subject areas. 'Education' is still an important area of postgraduate study and qualification for both women and men; indeed over 35 per cent of female postgraduates are found here and nearly a fifth of the men. Much the most common postgraduate route for men, however, is 'biological and physical sciences' accounting for over three in ten of them.

The high degree of concentration into a relatively small number of subjects is confirmed for both women and men. Nearly three-quarters of Welsh female postgraduates are in three of the ten lines – the other two, apart from education, being business, administration and social studies (21.5 per cent) and physical and biological science (15.1 per cent). Eighty-two per cent of the men are concentrated in four subjects (these being, in addition to education and science, engineering and technology, and administration, etc.).

In many of the subject areas, the balance of female to male Welsh postgraduates has become relatively even. Two subject areas stand out where women are still seriously under-represented in advanced university studies. One is in biological and physical sciences – 28 per cent are women – the other is, (of course), engineering and technology (11.4 per cent).

In the previous section concerned with undergraduates, we described measures of the relative over- and under-representation of Welsh women (and men) to UK students in different subject areas. The same comparisons are available for postgraduate students (Table A12). There are two main differences from the results relating to undergraduates. The extent of over- and under-representation is in general greater, though that is partly a reflection of the greater variation that comes with the smaller numbers involved. And Welsh women are not under-represented in the biological and physical sciences as they are among first degree students. There are still several subject areas characterised by Welsh female under-representation – medicine and health, as well as engineering and technology; administration, business, and social studies; other arts; and the multidisciplinary field. This shortfall is over 25 per cent in both medicine and health, and in engineering and technology. (The '+' signs in the table, signifying relative over-representation, are in the subject areas of education, architecture and other professional and vocational studies, and language and literature.)

In summary,

> Women have made inroads into the traditional male occupancy of postgraduate places and the female/male balance of Welsh students throughout the UK is now 44/56. There is a higher degree of concentration into particular subject areas among postgraduate than undergraduate students, with approximately three quarters of the female Welsh postgraduates in three of the ten subject lines, and over eight in ten of the males in four subject areas. The most significant imbalances are still in the sciences, with only 28 per cent women in biological and physical sciences and 11.4 per cent in engineering and technology. And, as is the case for undergraduates, Welsh female students are under-represented in engineering and technology compared with women throughout the UK, as they are in medicine and health (but not in this case in the biological and physical sciences).

Access courses

Access provision has proved to be an important opening towards educational opportunity for women in Wales; it is a 'second-chance' route to higher education for those who do not possess or who missed out on the normal academic qualifications that open access to advanced studies. They are especially valuable in being focused on adult needs and in being a non-traditional route that often leads to progression to higher education. Most FE colleges and about half the HE institutions in Wales operate an Access programme. Access courses have rapidly expanded; the increase in enrolments since 1988/89 has been ten-fold with numbers rising from 150 to 1509 in 1993/94. Progression to HE has risen over the past five years in Wales and nearly three-quarters of students now continue in this way (Wales Access Unit 1993, and communication with the Wales Access Unit).

Women have formed the majority of Access students throughout this period. While this has reduced somewhat since 1990, women still make up 58 per cent of the total in 1993/94 (down from 63 per cent in 1990/91). In addition to this numerical advantage, some provision has been specifically targeted to women in the areas of IT and technology where, as elsewhere, they are under-represented (Wales Access Unit 1993, p. 2).

An audit in North Wales for the academic year 1991/92 (Griffiths 1992), was based on a survey of Access students comprising over three-quarters women. The study is useful in shedding additional light on the Welsh language issue. The findings in this regard are complex: a small (2.5 per cent) group indicated their preference for all-Welsh medium courses even though 10 per cent had declared Welsh to be their preferred language of conversation. An earlier study of Access students who had proceeded to higher education found similar if slightly lower proportions of women (two-thirds) in 1991 (Lodge et al. 1991), and a modal age group in their thirties, with relatively low previous qualifications that normally would not have permitted enrolment in a full HE programme. This study did find, however, that Access students proceeded to a sub-set of HE courses rather than to the full range: 'all respondents who indicated their degree subject were studying in the Humanities, Law, or Social Science fields' (p. 4). The issue of breadth of access has thus still to be fully resolved, though the Wales Access Unit report does suggest that subject choice is broadening over time.

In summary,

> Students on Access programmes have expanded ten-fold between 1988/89 and 1993/94 and such courses are now widely available throughout FE and, increasingly, in HE. Approximately three-quarters progress in Wales to HE. Women have always constituted the majority of Access students, and are now 58 per cent of the students following this route. The issue of breadth of access to HE has still to be fully resolved, in particular opening up routes to science degrees.

The Open University

Many of the same patterns as elsewhere in higher education are in evidence for Open University (OU) undergraduates in Wales (Table A13). Considering undergraduate course registrations, the recent trend is towards a slightly more even overall gender balance from 40.9 per cent women in 1990 to attain 43.2 per cent by 1992. Six in ten of these female OU registrations are in the arts and social sciences, whereas 53.9 per cent of the equivalent males are found in mathematics and technology. Just as in mainstream university settings, these latter programmes still do not attract enough women students. The proportions of women in mathematics and technology were 22.1 per cent and 13 per cent respectively. These are smaller percentages than for men in the traditional female domains of arts and education; these stood at 33.7 per cent and 26.1 per cent respectively.

52

Concerning the age distribution of these students (Table A14), this form of distance learning is more successful in attracting older women than older men. Over six in ten (62.2 per cent in 1992) among the male students were under 40 years of age compared with 43.4 per cent of the female students.

In summary,

> The gender patterns of overall enrolment and subject choice in the Open University align closely with those in conventional university programmes. This may be regarded as unexpected, given the propensity of women to study in open and distance programmes in FE, and given the female majority in Access programmes. The 'male' programmes attract fewer women than the 'female' programmes do men. This form of distance learning is, however, more successful in attracting older women than older men.

Women and teaching: initial training and college lecturers

In this report our focus on teachers does not extend to the inequalities of recruitment and promotion among schoolteachers. It is, in looking specifically at the position of women in post-school education and training in Wales, on the dual aspects of women as student teachers and of patterns relating to the academic staff who teach in further and higher education. The patterns revealed are especially important insofar as marked gender inequalities among teachers reinforce those among students and trainees. The findings confirm these concerns; in initial teacher training, men are much more likely than women to be on postgraduate rather than undergraduate programmes; and the patterns of promotions among lecturers are very unequal indeed. Of particular concern is the evidence that these inequalities are still greater in the University of Wales than they are in British universities in general.

Initial teacher training

Approximately three-quarters of the enrolments in initial teacher training in Wales are women (74 per cent in 1991/92), and this is slightly up on earlier years (Table A7). The men who do undertake teacher training are more likely than women to be on a Postgraduate Certificate of Education (PGCE) programme than the undergraduate BEd degree programmes. Four in ten of male students in initial teacher training are on a PGCE and they comprise a similar proportion on these programmes compared with women. The female patterns are thus quite different; only 22 per cent of the women initial teacher trainees are at the postgraduate level, while they make up nearly eight in ten of the BEd enrolments. Later differences in teaching posts and marked gender inequalities in patterns of promotion are thus already foreshadowed in initial training.

The age distributions of first-year teacher trainees reflect these differences, given that postgraduates must be older than many of the undergraduates who are immediate school-leavers (Table A8). In fact, teaching seems to represent a field for 'male returners' looking for a new career just as it does for 'female returners' coming back to the classroom. For whereas the overall balance of women to men among first-year students is 70/30 (56/44 in universities), it is significantly lower among the older students: 52/48 for the 25–29 year-olds and 60/40 for the over-30 age group (the corresponding figures in universities are 42/58 and 50/50 respectively).

In summary,

> Consideration of the situation regarding teacher training and teachers/lecturers is especially important insofar as marked gender inequalities among teachers reinforce those in evidence among students and trainees. Women are the clear majority among students in initial teacher training in Wales, but whereas they dominate in BEd courses (eight in ten students) the balance is much more even in PGCE programmes (60/40 female/male). Otherwise put, only a fifth of women teacher trainees are in the postgraduate programmes. Partly as a reflection of this, but also possibly as teaching is a field for male mid-career change, female dominance is much less apparent among the older students in initial training.

Teachers and managers in FE and HE – very few women in promoted posts in Wales

Regarding the teaching staff in FE and HE, the dearth of women is clearcut, despite the relative equality of numbers among students (Table A15). Men substantially outnumber women and make up over two-thirds of the lecturers and senior staff in FE and non-university HE. Still more starkly unequal are the management appointments. Men comprised approximately 90 per cent of the 38 Welsh Principals (89.5 per cent), 86.7 per cent of the Principal Lecturers and over three-quarters of the Senior Lecturers. Despite very modest inroads by women into these promoted posts between 1990 and 1992, the concentration of women academics and teachers as unpromoted lecturers has altered little from the 77.4 per cent in 1990 as it remains just above three-quarters at 76.1 per cent of women. This is in contrast with 61.7 per cent of their male colleagues in 1992.

If anything, the evidence relating to the university sector (University of Wales only) gives greater grounds for concern. For in this case (Table A16), comparisons can be drawn with the averages for universities across Great Britain as a whole. The main patterns replicate those described above for the FE and non-university HE sectors; only 2.5 per cent of Professors in the University of Wales were women at the end of 1992 and the position was little better for Readers and Senior Lecturers at 5.5 per cent. Though the representation of women among senior academic staff across Great Britain as a whole is not dramatically different, it is definitely more favourable for women. The corresponding percentages to those above are in this case 5.1 per cent and 11 per cent, more than double the Welsh figures. And *among* female academics, whereas in Wales only 7.4 per cent had attained the posts of Professor, Reader or Senior Lecturer, the corresponding GB overall percentage was 12.2 per cent.

Moreover, compared with the approximate 30/70 female/male balance of all teachers in FE and non-university HE, in the university sector less than one in five of the teaching and research staff in Wales are female (18.8 per cent).

In summary,

> Men still well outnumber women in lectureships and especially in management positions in HE and FE in Wales despite the relative sex equality in student numbers. About seven in ten posts are held by men. In the university sector it is more than eight in ten. The pattern of inequality is linear with seniority – less than a quarter of Senior Lecturers were women in 1992 and women held only about one in ten of the management posts outside of universities. This falls to little over one in 20 Readers and Senior Lecturers in the university sector and a mere one in 40 of the Chairs. While these patterns are repeated across universities in Britain, the share of women in the higher academic posts in Wales is significantly lower.

Other education and training for adults

Wales behind on National Targets for Education and Training (formerly National Education and Training Targets): women well behind in vocational qualifications

The evidence on other forms of public and enterprise-based training can usefully be understood in the context of the need for a training drive in Wales in order to break out of the perpetuating circles that sustain a 'low-wage/low-skill' economy. The particularities of the Welsh economy and the place of women in it were addressed in the previous chapter; key aspects include the historical concentration of employment in a small number of industrial sectors – agriculture, coal, and steel – which have collapsed as mainstays of the economy; very high labour force inactivity, sickness, and disability levels in Wales; and the trends in employment towards low-skill services, part-time jobs, and depressed wage levels. These changes all affect women inordinately.

But far from this problematic combination leading to a massive training drive in order to make good the deficit, the evidence indicates that Wales is near or at the bottom of the cross-Britain comparisons. For example, the recently published 'report on progress' towards the achievement of the National Targets for Education and Training (NTETs) by the National Advisory Council for Education and Training Targets (NACETT) shows that, of the countries of the UK in 1993, Wales is the easily the lowest in the proportion of 19 year-olds achieving the Foundation Target (FT) 1 – i.e. at least NVQ level 2 or equivalent (NACETT 1994, Annex 1, Table 1). Compared with the UK average on FT1 of 61 per cent, 58 per cent attained this level in Wales. A regional analysis by gender is not included in the report, but the English patterns can be expected to be replicated, if not exaggerated, in Wales.

In summary,

> In England, girls continue to out perform boys at GCSE (by about seven percentage points). But overall, 4 per cent fewer girls than boys are reaching the Foundation Target 1 level. This implies that the proportion of girls achieving level 2 vocational qualifications is about two-thirds that of boys. The Council believes that further research on girls' take-up of vocational qualifications is needed so that those responsible for the development of GNVQs and NVQs can take early action to address this apparent imbalance. (p.17)

Wales is not only behind the other UK countries in the proportion of 21 year-olds achieving Foundation Target 3 (i.e. at least NVQ level 3 or equivalent) – though Northern Ireland is only marginally better in this regard – but it is below all the English regions as well (NACETT 1994, Annex 1, Table 7). The Welsh percentage in this case is 31 per cent as against a UK average – which includes the low Welsh figures – of 37 per cent (ibid. pp. 23, 65). Again, gender breakdowns are not available in the regional analysis, but the situation in England gives cause for still greater concern as regards women's access to and take-up of vocational education and training (VET) than in the case of Foundation Target 1 described above.

56

There is a significant difference – of ten percentage points – between the overall achievement levels of young men and women. Comparison of their respective GCE A level achievements suggests that, compared with males, comparatively few females are pursuing and succeeding in level 3 vocational qualifications. Also, there is a wider gap between males and females at level 3 than at level 2. This suggests that fewer females who could benefit are successfully undertaking level 3 courses. It is clear that – as part of the drive to strengthen vocational routes – more should be done to make suitable vocational qualifications available to, and attractive to, young women so as to encourage them to continue their education and training beyond level 2. (p. 25)

Given that Wales lags well behind England and Scotland in its achievement of FT3, it is only to be expected that the situation of young women is even worse than described for England in the NACETT Progress Report.

In summary,

Wales lags behind the other countries of the UK in the proportions attaining the National Targets for Education and Training at the Foundation levels. Compared with the UK average for Foundation level 1 of 61 per cent of 19 year-olds, the Welsh figure is 58 per cent; the corresponding percentages for Foundation level 3 are 37 and 31. As regards FT3, Wales is not only behind the other countries of the UK, but behind all the English regions as well. Though gender breakdowns are not available by region, in England a major problem is identified to be the shortfall in young women attaining vocational qualifications. It is only to be expected that the situation is, if anything, worse in Wales.

A poor record in enterprise-related training

It might be hoped that the relatively poor showing of Wales in its attainment of the Foundation Targets of NTETs, which are defined in terms of qualifications achieved by young adults, might be compensated for by later job-related training received by older adults through the workplace. Unfortunately, not only does Wales again show up poorly in regional comparisons (Table 4.4), but women in Wales do particularly badly (Table 4.5). The regional comparisons permitted by the Labour Force Survey (Department of Employment 1993) confirm the poor Welsh performance, taking men and women together.

Table 4.4 **Percentage of the population of working age receiving job-related training in the four weeks prior to the survey, by TEED region, 1992**

Region/country	%
Great Britain	9.9
South East	10.8
London	10.0
South West	9.8
West Midlands	9.7
East Midlands	9.2
Eastern	10.6
Yorkshire and Humberside	9.7
Greater Manchester	9.9
North West	9.6
Northern	9.8
Scotland	9.3
WALES	8.6

Source: Department of Employment (1993a) Table B21.

Table 4.5 **Percentage of employees of working age receiving job-related training in the four weeks prior to the survey, by gender and GB region, 1992**

Region/country	All	Men	Women	M–W
Great Britain	14.5	14.4	14.7	−0.3
South East	15.7	15.5	16.0	−0.5
South West	14.2	13.9	14.5	−0.6
West Midlands	14.2	13.9	14.7	−0.8
East Midlands	13.1	12.3	14.1	−1.8
East Anglia	13.6	13.9	13.2	+ 0.7
Yorkshire and Humberside	14.0	14.1	14.0	+ 0.1
North West	14.9	14.5	15.2	−0.7
North	14.3	14.6	14.0	+0.6
Scotland	13.4	13.7	13.0	+0.7
WALES	13.4	14.2	12.5	+1.8

Source: Department of Employment (1993a) Table B16.

The Welsh figure, at 8.6 per cent, is the lowest of any of the regional GB comparisons. In referring to *all* adults of working age, it is possible that factors other than low relative opportunities for training in and through firms are reflected in this poor showing. That is, these figures might be influenced by such structural differences as the higher incidence of self-employment or of economic inactivity in Wales, which might serve to depress the incidence of job-related training among all adults. Yet, when *employees* are taken as the basis of comparison, Wales does little better, especially female employees.

In fact, the incidence of job-related training among women in Wales is nineteenth out of the 20 gender-specific regional training rates in the table. Only men in the East Midlands experience a lower training rate.

The second significant aspect of the table concerns the differences between the incidence of training between male and female employees. In the majority of the cases indicated in the table, the women's training rate is higher than men's (though the table indicates nothing about the level or quality of the job-related training in question). In a minority of the regions, however, this pattern is reversed as in Scotland and the Northern region of England. Not only is this also the case in Wales, but the male advantage in percentage terms is much the most significant of any included in the table.

In summary,

> It might be hoped that the relatively poor showing of Wales in its attainment of the Foundation Targets of NTETs, which are defined in terms of qualifications achieved by young adults, might be compensated for by later job-related training received through work by older adults. Unfortunately, not only does Wales again show up poorly in regional comparisons, but women in Wales do particularly badly. Their incidence of job-related training is not only the worst compared with women in any of the other GB regions, but the gap in this regard between men and women is also the largest in these regions.

Career Development Loans

Career Development Loans (CDL) are a relatively recent feature of vocational education and training (VET) in Britain. Their purpose is to provide financial assistance to those wishing to undertake VET but are otherwise unable to raise the funds for the purpose. At the time of writing, these loans are administered nationally through the Department of Employment, rather than locally through the TECs. Eligible training can last anything between one week and one year, and the loans may be from £300 to £5,000 (Career Development Loans 1993).

In 1992/93, 413 CDLs were awarded in Wales. Women comprised only 37 per cent of these. The gender balance was more even among the younger age groups: 43 per cent of the 21 years and below age group, and 45.3 per cent of those aged 22–24 years. The disparity is much wider among the next band aged 25–39 – the modal age range – where only 34 per cent of the successful applicants in Wales were women in 1992/93. This fell still more to less than 30 per cent among the 40–54 year age group. The value of the loans awarded was on average slightly higher for women than for men: £2,996.04 and £2,942.11 respectively (Communication with the Department of Employment).

In summary,

> To date, more men than women in Wales have successfully applied for Career Development Loans; of the 413 awarded in 1992/93, 37 per cent went to women. The imbalance is particularly marked among older applicants and trainees.

Public training interventions

The Employment Training (ET) programme for adult long-term unemployed was renamed Training for Work in 1993. It represents the main form of publicly-sponsored training for the adult unemployed and aims at enhancing activity and employability through skills development. Like YT, it is administered by the TECs. Comparisons of levels of participation in this form of training can prove to be misleading when that participation is determined by a complex mix of demand and supply, rather than any single factor. Though participation rates themselves can be expected to vary for many reasons, the proportion of those participating who achieve a vocational qualification does provide a more meaningful basis of comparison. Once again, Wales does not figure well in these comparisons, as the share of ET trainees who achieved a qualification in 1992 was, at 29 per cent, lower in Wales not only than the English average but the percentage for all the English regions as well (Central Statistical Office 1993, Table 7.21). The differences are nevertheless relatively modest in this case.

Data relevant to different gender experiences are patchy and unable at present to provide a picture for Wales as a whole. The statistics collected by individual TECs offer some insights but these remain at best illustrative without more systematic compilation and presentation of the statistics (the following paragraphs are based on communications with individual TECs). In North East Wales, for instance, the quarterly figures show men make up between 80 and 85 per cent of the Training for Work starts. The balance is slightly more even in South Glamorgan, albeit still with men comprising three-quarters of the starts in adult training. But women appear more likely than men to translate this form of skills development and retraining into tangible outcomes: a third or more of the South Glamorgan trainees finding jobs were women in the recent period. More data are needed through which to assess the gender distribution of take-up of and outcomes from this form of publicly-sponsored skills training, and research could usefully shed light on the extent to which the female long-term unemployed receive training and the outcomes that follow from it.

What also emerges from the sketchy data is the degree to which this form of training is sharply segregated along gender lines. It is not a linear segregation in that, given the very wide differences between numbers of men and women trainees altogether, there are more 'male' fields where women rarely train than there are 'female' occupational domains with no men.

The North West Wales TEC, TARGED, supplied Training for Work half-yearly breakdowns by occupational classification up to September 1993. Of the 25 occupational groups (with sub-divisions giving 27), there were no trainees at all in five of these in this period. Of the 22 with trainees, ten were all male. Two of the remaining 12 were all female, but these represented only five trainees in all. Though in some of these cases the numbers are too few to allow valid comparisons, in other occupational fields these findings of marked gender segregation are founded on a more solid basis of numbers of trainees. Mid Glamorgan TEC also supplied some indication of patterns in this regard and in this case the absolute numbers are greater. Of the 21 adult training occupational fields in December 1993, five were exclusively male, and women trainees were 5 per cent or less in another four.

In summary,

> Though the data on Employment Training (ET) and its successor programme, Training for Work, are weak and not collected or presented in a consistent way across Wales, those available suggest that many more men participate than women. This does not necessarily lead to positive outcomes, and Wales again does relatively poorly compared with other parts of Britain, in this case through comparisons of the proportions of trainees who achieve a vocational qualification through their training. Occupational segregation and traditional choices remain very marked, especially in the 'male' fields.

Adult education

This section reports evidence prior to the incorporation of the FE colleges described earlier, and the changes which have removed substantial areas of post-school education from local authority control. (Thus adult education programmes are here described as being provided in 'LEA adult education centres', Table A17.) Though the governance of education has been subject to a radical shake-up, we can expect patterns of enrolment in adult education to be more stable. Change might be expected in the event of any subsequent shift in emphasis from non-vocational to vocational adult provision. In 1991/92, many more women than men undertook adult education at LEA centres in Wales, much (though not all) in non-vocational programmes of various sorts (Table A17). Nearly 73 per cent of overall enrolments were women, and of these many more (seven in ten) were for evening programmes. Of the part-time day adult education enrolments, eight in ten were women.

The picture is far from uniform in this regard across Wales. Enrolments as a percentage of the adult population were far higher in South Glamorgan, containing the city of Cardiff, than in any other county at nearly 9 per cent, with the next highest enrolment per capita of the adult population in Gwent at a little over 5 per cent (Welsh Office 1993a, Figure 14). Powys, at 2 per cent, West Glamorgan at slightly less, and Gwynedd at less than 1 per cent are the lowest. While the urban/ rural dimension is clearly an important one in accounting for these differences, that alone does not offer a full explanation, given the relatively high participation rate in rural Dyfed and the poor position of West Glamorgan which contains the city of Swansea. Nor are the gender patterns of participation, as opposed to overall supply and demand in adult education, explicable in terms of rural and urban differences, as shown by Table 4.6.

Table 4.6   Enrolments at adult education centres, by LEA and gender, 1991/92

County	Females %	Males %	Total N
Clwyd	70.7	29.3	8,245
Dyfed	75.3	24.7	8,961
Gwent	77.5	22.5	14,598
Gwynedd	66.9	33.1	1,225
Mid Glamorgan	71.3	28.7	12,582
Powys	77.1	22.9	1,391
South Glamorgan	70.5	29.5	21,725
West Glamorgan	74.3	25.7	3,980
WALES	72.9	27.1	72,707

Source: Welsh Office 1993a, Table 10.3.

There is a wide variation between the Welsh counties in the female participation rate, with the highest in the South East Wales county of Gwent. That this is no simple urban/rural divide is shown by comparisons of two of the most rural counties. One of the highest rates of female involvement in adult education in 1991/92 was found in Powys (77.1 per cent); the lowest across the Welsh counties, on the other hand, was in Gwynedd at 66.9 per cent.

In summary,

> At least up to 1991/92, many more women than men participated in municipal adult education – nearly three-quarters of the adult learners in these courses in Wales. The rate is even higher among those who are day-time students, at eight in ten. Cardiff and South Glamorgan – the most urbanised parts of Wales – display much the highest participation per adult member of the population. Involvement in adult education and gender patterns do not, however, fit a simple model of urban/rural difference as one of the highest and the lowest female rates are found in rural counties.

Educational attainment of the adult population: high-level qualifications

Educational attainment of the total adult population gives a different perspective on patterns, problems and needs. Since adults across the age range are included, the patterns revealed often relate to practices and experiences from well in the past rather than contemporary outflows from higher education. Thus, while in the most recent years, women have caught up with men in the numbers acquiring university first degrees, for instance, the qualification levels of the total population reflect past practices and are still markedly unequal. Altogether in 1991 (Census data), a significantly higher proportion of men than women over 18 years old are qualified to diploma level or above in Wales (13.1 per cent compared with 10.9 per cent). This is a combination of more men holding such qualifications (13,482 compared with 12,372) and of the fact of greater numbers of women than men in the adult population (113,408 women and 102,639 men). More men in Wales hold degrees, whether undergraduate or postgraduate, for all age groups. Whereas these differences are much reduced for the youngest 18–30 age group for first-level degrees (52.3 per cent compared with 47.7 per cent) than among older members of the Welsh population, they are still very marked among postgraduate degree holders of all ages, including young adults. Among higher education diploma level graduates, on the other hand, women outnumber men in all the age groups calculated in the Census and are 58.7 per cent of diploma graduates averaged across all age groups.

Table 4.7 shows the county breakdowns. The differences in the advanced qualification levels of men and women are not large comparing one county with another in Wales; all conform broadly to the pattern of women making up approximately a quarter of higher degree holders, while comprising 35–40 per cent of first-degree graduates. On the other hand, nearly six in ten of those with higher education diplomas at sub-degree level in Wales were women in 1991.

Table 4.7   **All-Wales and county percentages of the 1991 10 per cent sample Census for adults with (a) higher degrees, (b) undergraduate degrees, and (c) university diplomas, by gender**

County		Total N	Female %	Male %	
Clwyd	a	165	24.2	75.8	
	b	1,287	35.7	64.3	
	c	2,066	58.4	41.6	
Dyfed	a	213	25.4	74.6	
	b	1,351	37.7	62.3	
	c	1,808	62.7	37.3	
Gwent	a	129	18.6	81.4	
	b	1,489	36.3	63.7	
	c	2,060	55.4	44.6	
Gwynedd	a	182	23.6	76.4	
	b	1,002	36.3	63.7	
	c	1,284	62.5	37.5	
Mid Glamorgan	a	138	23.9	76.1	
	b	1,360	34.8	65.2	
	c	2,233	56.3	43.7	
Powys	a	57	24.6	75.4	
	b	485	38.8	61.2	
	c	615	63.6	36.4	
South Glamorgan	a	413	24.5	75.5	
	b	2,399	39.6	60.4	
	c	2,017	57.7	42.3	
West Glamorgan	a	202	26.2	73.8	
	b	1,312	38.0	62.0	
	c	1,587	58.6	41.4	
WALES	a	1,499	24.1	75.9	
	b	10,685	37.3	62.7	
	c	13,670	58.7	41.3	

Source: OPCS 1994, Table 84.

Gwent and Mid Glamorgan stand out as the counties in Wales where women are less well qualified in comparison to men. The female–male balance is lower than the Welsh average for each of the qualification levels for both of these counties.

These findings put a different emphasis on the education and training policy issues confronting women in Wales than many of the others presented in this chapter. They show that, whatever the change over recent years in female access to learning opportunities (which we have seen has been marked in some areas and modest in others), these have affected the younger generations much more than older adults. Continuing education and training is thus a priority if these inequalities are to be redressed. This is especially important in the light of developments away from unskilled jobs and efforts to encourage advanced technology investment in Wales. These will leave older women in particular at a still greater disadvantage unless the focus on the initial systems of skills development is complemented by priority too for continuing education and training opportunities.

In summary,

> Many more men in Wales possess university degree-level qualifications than women. While for undergraduate degrees the difference is sharply reduced among the younger age categories, far less reduction is in evidence for post-graduate degrees. More women than men possess 'sub-degree' level HE diplomas. These patterns hold across the counties of Wales; the female disadvantage compared with men is most apparent in Gwent and Mid Glamorgan. These findings emphasise the importance of continuing education and training in realising equal opportunities.

4.4   STATISTICS AND MONITORING

The importance of statistics that are accessible, comprehensive, and consistent

Given the many pages of statistics that have been reviewed in this chapter, the call for more and better statistics may seem at first sight to be misplaced. But there are many gaps. There are types of education and training where data are not gathered which would allow women's prospects more accurately to be identified. There are many detailed examples where the records of institutions, providers and agencies are such that breakdowns are possible in principle, but where these are not exploited in the statistics that enter into the public arena. There are some areas of education and training provision where the variation in practice in the classification and compilation of records is very wide such that the gender monitoring that could be conducted on the basis of the 'best practice' of particular institutions or counties could not be repeated to reveal a comprehensive picture. And there are the repeated changes in the organisation and governance of education and training that disrupt both the establishment of trends and the responsibilities for generating and producing the data on which progress or deterioration can be established. In short, the improvement of statistics in order to permit gender monitoring is a multi-faceted operation with a number of key dimensions.

The *form* in which statistics are presented can make a substantial difference to their value for the purposes of gender monitoring. A few of the statistical tables included in this chapter and Appendix III are reproduced in their original form. In the large majority of cases, however, a major exercise of re-analysis has been required in order to convert raw numbers into the percentages that allow the gender distributions to emerge with clarity. Even where the data that permit the identification of the situation of women in education and training exist, therefore, the issue of their *accessibility* is to the fore. We recognise that in general compendia of statistics, patterns and trends relating to women and men are only one among various aspects of interest. Even granted this, we would still expect as a minimum that when breakdowns by gender are included in tables that they are calculated and presented in a usable form rather than necessitating substantial secondary analysis in order to be understood.

Accessibility has another dimension, more general in application, in addition to that of improving the comprehensibility of the tables in published compendia. This refers to the frequent drawing together of those regularly-compiled statistics on education and training so that the full picture on education, training and gender can be acquired in a single source. To be effective, once such a source is designed on an agreed format, there should be the commitment to continue it on an annual basis.

This report represents the start of such an exercise on an all-Wales basis, but it does not fully meet the aims outlined above. This is because our report has been produced on a one-off basis rather than as the first in a continuing series designed to track the position of women in post-school education and training. More specifically, it is both broader in scope and more preliminary in its contents than the format we have in mind for monitoring purposes. That would call for the development of a set of agreed indicators, based on existing statistics or the generation of new ones where necessary, that would then constitute the gender 'scorecard' for Wales annually. *Accessibility* in this sense means availability of consistent and comprehensive statistics to a wide audience of interested parties, including those in the education and training worlds, but also in firms, voluntary organisations, different branches of government, community and interest groups, and the media, as well as interested individuals.

Indeed, we envisage that the production of such a detailed 'scorecard' would give much-needed impetus to the scrutiny of education and training statistics in Wales to assess their adequacy for the purposes of gender monitoring. It would stimulate the generation of improved data where gaps have been identified. The questions of the adequacy and generation of good statistics are highly detailed and technical, and so cannot be suggested in the generalities of this report. It requires a new and specific task, combining the energies and efforts of existing institutions and agencies.

Such an exercise would expose the wide variations in current county and institutional practices concerning which data by gender are generated and stored. It would also help to highlight those aspects of education and training where information, whether relating to gender or not, is presently very weak. Much more is known about enrolments in institutional settings that have traditionally constituted 'systems' of provision in the public domain – schools and colleges for example – than in settings which have been newly-established, decentralised in administration or disparate in organisation, or private in form. The practices and performances of providers in the 'market' for training, formally private though often dependent on public funds, are a case in point.

It is also obvious that the statistics and indicators in question might well extend far beyond enrolment and participation data to include such matters as completion, drop-out, destinations, and staffing. And within each of these areas, it will be important that the particular measures developed are appropriate as valid indicators and sensitive to considerations of gender.

Yet it is also important that the generation of data does not add to the bureaucratic burdens that already are onerous, and are exacerbated by the continual change in demands and formats in education and training. Hence again there is value in an agreed set of indicators rather than the production of mountains of information in the hope that by firing grapeshot some of the targets will be hit. Well-designed, integrated data management systems are especially important here.

Illustrative examples

A good illustration of an area where information of any kind, let alone that permitting gender patterns to be identified, is patchy or non-existent is of non-participation in education, training or employment by post-school teenagers – a crucial aspect of education and training if current youth policies are to be evaluated. A recent study of this phenomenon in South Wales identifies lack of data as especially problematic, and considers ways of improving this lack that apply as much to the subject of this report (Istance et al.1994):

> Many of our conclusions relate to the paucity of existing information and data. Improvement is thus a priority. It would, however, be costly and ineffective if this is interpreted to mean that *any* additional information is to be preferred willy-nilly over what is available at present. Very close attention is required to what is gathered, what information needs are and the adequacy of current production to meet these needs, the practical arrangements to ensure systematic data-gathering and proper co-ordination both with other agencies within the county and with similar services in other counties ... . Education and training data are especially weak ... (pp.17–18)

This need for improvement becomes still more pressing in the light of the increasing introduction of market arrangements, as good information is a prerequisite of an efficient market, and so that the success of those reforms will be open to evaluation.

Illustrative of the variations in existing statistical practices and their adequacy for gender monitoring are the replies we received from individual TECs. These included the following observations and remarks:

> We are in the process of developing a Management Information Return that will breakdown the data sufficiently to satisfy enquiries such as i)c and i)d so will be unable to answer those questions at present.

> It has not been possible within the timescale requested to provide more detailed information ...

> Most of this data [on gender take-up of public training] is not readily available from our management information system ... unfortunately our records on Enterprise and Management training are less accessible. This will not be the case for much longer. Basically, what we have tells you numbers of participants and not much else. Soon, however, our data should be similar and more robust throughout our programmes.
> (Welsh TEC information officers)

The general message, nevertheless, is that the management, consistency and comprehensiveness of institutional data are in the process of overhaul, and that present inadequacies should not be seen as indicative of persisting gaps.

A specific point to arise in our contacts with the TECs relates to YT and Adult Training starts, but is one with more wide-ranging significance. The returns from training providers on which these are based at present are 'one-dimensional' on each of the dimensions of sex, disability, field of training, employed status, etc. of trainees. This means that no combination or cross-tabulation is possible that would show how the male trainees are distributed across these other variables, on the one hand, and the women trainees, on the other. Were these limitations to be overcome to allow multidimensional analyses, important additional insights would be allowed. Again, integrated information systems, in which all training providers and the TEC are connected, promise significantly to extend these possibilities.

From the responses from the colleges, they appear to be better established and consistent in their data management, partly driven by requirements of regular submissions of returns to the Welsh Office and to the Funding Council. Some of them are able to respond swiftly and efficiently to the call on data and analysis that is made of them, including detailed breakdowns by gender.

There are nevertheless substantial variations in the detailed contents and form of college data. Catering for such a variety of courses and student/trainees, there is also the risk that gender monitoring is rendered confused by the sheer detail of the information held by the colleges. There is room here for the development of a standard format for gender monitoring for the colleges, uniform so as to allow comparisons across time and institution but sufficiently flexible to reflect the realities of FE/HE and local labour markets.

One specific aspect of college data where there are wide variations regards *destinations* data. Some, but not all, of the colleges follow their students and trainees into their first months post-college, and there is variation too in the detail with which information on women and men can be separated. This could usefully be standardised.

The mechanisms and context of data-gathering
An obvious danger of the repeated reorganisation of education and training, with growing diversity of provision and the devolution of responsibilities, is that each body might create data to suit its own perceived immediate needs or else give data management a lower priority as it struggles to meet the immediate requirements of teaching or training. These are understandable responses but they would serve badly the interests of education and training provision and of equal opportunities in Wales. Unless it is possible to establish benchmarks, identify problems, and chart progress towards equality of opportunity, a substantial mechanism of accountability is denied.

The trends towards 'marketisation' outlined in Chapter 2 might be expected to exacerbate variability, as each institution 'goes its own way'. That does not, however, appear to be happening. In fact, that very devolution has created new pressures for better, more unified information if chaos is to be avoided. Markets function on the basis of a 'currency', and a basic currency is precisely that of information. Instead of characterising the situation as one where there is a lack of statistical awareness, it is much more accurate to say that there is a growing awareness of statistical lack. In this context, our emphasis on the need for improved statistics and for better gender monitoring fits well with these other ongoing developments.

Given the need for comprehensiveness and consistency of data, co-ordination at the all-Wales level is vital, assuming that it is with the active involvement of all concerned, especially of the colleges and providers who will be responsible for data collection and local interpretation. As well as involvement by individual colleges, training providers and TECs, there are distinctive roles for various players in the process including, of course, the Welsh Office but also the relevant funding councils, the Council of Welsh TECs, the WDA, as well as specialist organisations with responsibilities for specific parts of the education and training systems in Wales or for particular student or trainee groups. As our focus here is essentially on the creation of a useful and durable system of data for gender monitoring, the EOC has its own special contribution to make.

5.   EDUCATION AND TRAINING INITIATIVES FOR WOMEN

5.1   INTRODUCTION

Wales is arguably well served by examples of innovative initiatives in the field of women's education and training, many of which have been pioneered by groups of women themselves. This section briefly describes some of those initiatives. The Equal Opportunities Commission recently published a handbook of good practice in women's training, **Realising Potential: Increasing the effectiveness of education and training provision for women, which draws upon various initiatives in Wales** (EOC/Chwarae Teg 1993). The purpose of the handbook is to increase the effectiveness of education and training for women. In compiling the handbook, a substantial trawl of projects was undertaken. The purpose of this section is not to replicate that handbook, but to draw attention to a small number of particularly noteworthy initiatives, and draw some general lessons from them.

However, it should be emphasised that although initiatives such as the ones described are most welcome, they are not a substitute for the comprehensive provision of education and training which addresses women's needs and thereby those of the economy in general.

2.2   EDUCATION AND TRAINING INITIATIVES

Opportunity 2000

Welsh subscribers to Opportunity 2000 include major employers in both the public and private sector such as Cardiff City Council, the National Health Service in Wales, NatWest, Lucas, Cwmbran, Iceland Frozen Foods and Welsh Water. While many of the subscribers are among the largest employers in Wales, small and medium-sized enterprises are also participating, such as Jennifer Griffiths Recruitment based in Bridgend and Neath. Those subscribers which have focused on training as a strategy to develop female human resources include Elac and Peters Savoury Products.

A major problem in Wales is the predominance of small and medium-sized enterprises which often lack the resources or flexibility to engage in some of the human resource activities now being pursued by larger organisations. Opportunity 2000 has set up a project whereby Welsh Water, one of the biggest indigenous Welsh companies, is mentoring a small company in Mid Glamorgan. There are plans to set up a similar mentoring project in North Wales in the near future.

Other activities supported by Opportunity 2000 in Wales include participation in the national 'Take Our Daughters to Work' day on 28 April 1994 and 'Take Our Employers to School' events in North and South Wales in June 1994. A seminar was recently held for construction firms in Wales to promote non-traditional areas of work and training.

South Glamorgan Women's Workshop

South Glamorgan Women's Workshop has recently celebrated ten years of providing tailor-made training for disadvantaged women in microcomputer technology, business computing and computer networking and telecommunications. All three courses include complementary studies aimed at personal and career development such as study and communication skills, and building self-confidence. The courses are certificated. Work placements help integrate women into the workforce and allow them to apply what they have learned in a work setting. It also gives employers an opportunity to see women returners working first-hand.

Set up by an independent group of women, the Workshop is largely financed by the ESF, South Glamorgan County Council, Cardiff City Council and Vale of Glamorgan Borough Council. The Workshop has achieved European renown for its pioneering work and has received awards for its work from national and European organisations.

The Workshop encourages applications from black, minority ethnic and disabled women. Outreach work with black and ethnic minority women encourages participation in courses with opportunities for progression. For example, an introductory course is run for minority ethnic women to prepare them for joining the year-long courses. Over the last five years, the Workshop has introduced courses for Asian women.

About 37 per cent of trainees are single parents, 75 per cent are not in paid employment and 38 per cent have no previous qualifications. An on-site nursery provides facilities for children from six weeks to five years, and hours are arranged to accommodate childcare responsibilities. No fees are charged.

The Workshop was designed with women's training needs as the main focus: the needs of disadvantaged women returners were scarcely catered for in mainstream training ten years ago. Since then, many of the practices have been 'mainstreamed', that is, adopted by other training providers. The Workshop has developed training in new areas where there are skill shortages in the local economy, such as advanced technologies and telecommunications skills (Fielder and T. Rees 1991). It has also developed its European links through membership of IRIS, the European Commission's network of women's training projects and through a participation in a New Opportunities for Women (NOW) project with transnational partners on telematics and telecommunications training for women returners (see below, and Essex et al. 1986; T. Rees 1992, 1993b).

Dove Workshop, Banwen

The Dove Workshop (Dulais Opportunity for Voluntary Support) is a community education and training centre in Banwen, on the northern edge of the coalfield in the Dulais Valley in West Glamorgan. It delivers a range of training courses on, for example, computing, film making and machine knitting. It was set up during the 1983/84 miners' strike by women from the Swansea, Neath and Dulais Valleys' Miners' support group as an attempt to keep the communities viable in the face of pit closures. The Dove Workshop represents a grass roots initiative drawing on the growing political activity engendered by the miners' strike, and increased confidence in women seeking to transfer their traditional skills into new arenas.

One of the keys to Dove's success in mobilising resources and delivering customised training to women in the community is its partnership approach. Links with the Department of Adult Continuing Education in University College, Swansea, which was seeking locally-based premises for its operations, facilitated the development of Dove into a project of standing within the European Union. It has partners in the IRIS network, which now include projects from other coal mining regions such as Sardinia and Belgium (see p. 77).

A main feature of Dove's activities has been guidance and counselling work. This has been offered to a wide section of the community, and throughout the training programme. Guidance is combined with regional labour market information, equal opportunities legislation and employment law. Hence:

> With this help, individuals, especially long term unemployed women, were seen
> to be empowered to make beneficial changes in their lives.
> (Francis and Pudner 1994, p. 6)

Community University of the Valleys

The 'Community University of the Valleys' which brings higher education into ex-mining South Wales Valley communities from University College Swansea's Department of Adult Continuing Education, is attracting women and men into second chance education based in their own localities. Resources (£200,000) from the Commission of the European Communities were used to convert old Coal Board buildings in Banwen into class rooms, a crèche, a library and a computer laboratory (the Centre is shared with the Dove workshop for women and Onllwyn Council). A minibus brings students in from outlying villages, and staff travel up the valley from University College Swansea to deliver classes. In this, the first year of operation, three Part One courses on Modern Welsh Studies, Modern European Studies and Environmental Studies were taught. Additional Part One and Part Two courses will be on offer next session.

There are no formal entry requirements but commitment and enthusiasm are important entry criteria. Fees are kept low and subsidies made available for the unemployed. Open University style credits are awarded which can be built up to an ordinary degree in five years: two further credits are required for an honours degree. The University guidance service is made available.

The biggest take-up has been from women, including some local single parents for whom only this tailor-made arrangement has made higher education a possibility. Of the first cohort of 22 students, 15 are women. Whereas the men are all over 40, the women's ages range from 24 to 62, with an average of 38 years. Most of the students had left full-time education at 15 or 16, and had no or few educational qualifications beyond GCSE.

The Community University of the Valleys hopes to expand numbers next year and bring higher education to people who would never be able to participate in existing courses on campus. The geographical difficulties, together with the cost and problems of childcare, would make taking up a degree place impossible. This project is the first community university initiative of its kind in the UK and others are expected to follow; it has received widespread coverage in both the Welsh and British media (see, for example, Coleman 1994; Road 1994; Smith 1993).

Valleys Women's Roadshow

The Valleys Women's Roadshow was developed as the result of collaboration between the Department of Adult Continuing Education at University College Swansea's 'Valleys Initiative for Adult Education', the Equal Opportunities Commission and Chwarae Teg. An application was made initially to the Welsh Office and the TECs in the area for a feasibility phase. Set up in April 1993, it is now independently managed and is funded by the Welsh Office and the County Councils of Dyfed, Gwent, Mid Glamorgan and West Glamorgan via the former Urban Programme. Its aim is to 'raise awareness of training and education opportunities for women, highlight the needs and barriers facing women, support and encourage women in gaining access to learning opportunities and work in partnership to widen opportunities for women'. The Roadshow's mission statement is: 'Working in partnership, to empower women in order to enrich the quality of life and to promote the regeneration of communities in the South Wales Valleys' (Valleys Women's Roadshow leaflet).

A key element in the Roadshow approach then is the context of the decline of heavy industry and mining in the valleys economy. This has meant the development of a new industrial base which, while not replacing the lost male jobs, has opened up opportunities for women in the labour market. Economic activity rates for women as a consequence have increased while those of men have decreased (see ERES 1994).

The development of new opportunities in the labour force for women is to be welcomed, but the jobs are often low-paid, part-time and unskilled or semi-skilled. Employers have reported that difficulties have been experienced because of the low educational level and lack of vocational qualifications of the female workforce. As discussed in Chapter 3, women's lack of confidence and erosion of skills through years at home with domestic responsibilities make the return to work difficult.

The purpose of the Roadshow is to address these issues through improving information flows about education and training opportunities to women whose networks do not allow them to access that information. Networks have been established and monthly events are staged across the Valleys with exhibitions from local education and training providers and local role models. Careers guidance is a crucial part of the project; in those counties where there is an established adult guidance service, this is utilised. A team of six women was appointed for three years. A management group is made up of representatives from the County Councils, TECs and education providers.

University of Wales College of Cardiff Bilingual Skills Training Project
The Department of Continuing Education at University of Wales College of Cardiff has been training qualified interpreters in the public services on a project funded by the Nuffield Interpreter

Project. The 20-week certificate course in public service interpreting began in December 1993 and trained eight women and seven men. The aim of the project is to create a bridge between members of various ethnic minorities in South Glamorgan and public service providers such as social services and the courts. The course creates an opportunity to facilitate bilingual members of ethnic minority groups to improve their translating and interpreting skills and gain a recognised qualification. It also provides an opportunity for progression through moving on to further recognised translation and interpretation qualifications. The Barnardo's Multi-cultural Resource Centre in Cardiff has also been successful in increasing educational opportunities for women from black and ethnic minority communities (EOC/Chwarae Teg 1993, p. 7).

South Wales Employers' Workshop
As important as improving training opportunities for women is developing employers' awareness of the complexities of equal opportunities on gender, race and disability, and developing policies to tackle direct and indirect discrimination. Following a Commission for Racial Equality survey of Cardiff employers (which showed the under-representation of ethnic minorities in employment), the South Wales Employers' Workshop of 40 employers was set up to provide informal advice and information for employers, especially on racial equality. The Workshop arranges training sessions on how to progress equal opportunities action plans, best practice in recruitment and selection, positive action, targeting, monitoring and combatting racial and sexual harassment. The group has support from the South Glamorgan Racial Equality Council which has recently seconded a development worker to it.

NOW Projects and the IRIS Network
The New Opportunities for Women (NOW) programme is funded by the European Commission under the ESF to encourage women to participate fully in the labour market and develop their skills. The projects are meant as demonstration projects from which good practice can be learned. A major feature of NOW projects is transnational partnership in learning. Applicants have to find matching funding from other sources.

There are seven NOW projects in Wales in the 1992/94 round. Gwent County Council is running a Women's Enterprise Resource Centre and has partners in Spain and Greece. Powys County Council has a Rural Access Initiative to stimulate training, education and progression of women workers in rural areas with partners in Denmark, Spain and the Netherlands. It is collaborating with Chwarae Teg in seeking to widen the role of women in the workforce in North and rural Wales. St

David's College Lampeter is running a project on women and country craft co-operatives in rural areas and has partners in Ireland and France. South Glamorgan Women's Workshop has a transnational returning-to-work project with partners in Ireland and Germany. The telematics and telecommunications vocational training project for women returners in computer networking run by South Glamorgan Women's Workshop has already been mentioned (see p. 73); the project has ten European partners. Finally, Swansea College is organising a project developing a new approach to health care, and has partners in Greece and Ireland.

The European Commission has announced that funding for a new round of NOW projects will be available from 1995 for a six-year period. The guidelines are currently being prepared.

There are six members of IRIS, the European Commission's network of women's training projects in Wales. They are South Glamorgan Women's Workshop, Cardiff (new technology and telematics and telecommunications), the Dove workshop at Banwen (women in technology), St David's University College Centre for Continuing Education at Lampeter (new technologies), North East Wales Institute on Deeside (science and technology); North East Wales Training and Enterprise Council Ltd (project on women in non-traditional engineering) and Gorseinon College (employment in training for women returners).

Women's Studies and Project Grace

Women's Studies courses have mushroomed in Wales as elsewhere in the UK. A recent HMI report claimed that they 'make a significant contribution to widening access to higher education, attracting mature women with non-standard qualifications' (EOC/Chwarae Teg 1993, p. 8). The first MSc in Women's Studies in Wales was taught at University of Wales College of Cardiff in the late 1980s; since then courses have appeared at undergraduate and postgraduate level in most of the FE/HE institutions. It is also an important element of access courses.

Project Grace, a HEFCW-funded initiative, has brought together those involved in teaching Women's Studies in the Principality, from access courses to higher degree work, to prepare course materials on women's history in Wales. The series of course units prepared by the project comprise text, commentary and bibliographies, including original sources. The units, published in July 1994 in both Welsh and English, are available as a resource for women's studies teaching, and for teaching about women in Wales on other pre-degree courses.

This is an important innovation in that pedagogic moves towards project-based work have been hampered by the lack of material on women in Wales. As Beddoe (1986, p. 227) has commented, women are culturally invisible in Wales. Students will now be able to draw upon this set of inexpensive and accessible units for flexible learning, wherever they live. They can be used at different levels.

Project Grace is also an innovative example of co-operation across the FE/HE divide, and on an all-Wales basis. Making available materials that are seen as relevant to women's lives and their interests, particularly for access students and those wishing to focus on Wales, is a valuable asset.

5.3   LESSONS FROM WOMEN'S EDUCATION AND TRAINING INITIATIVES

A major feature of these and many other initiatives is that they tend to be started by women for women, in recognition of the gaps or inappropriateness of mainstream provision. It is important to sustain these initiatives, while seeking to mainstream elements of good practice.

The projects are invariably funded on a shoe-string, with major energies being diverted from training to seeking further funding. It is important to secure more permanent funding for some of these projects, and provide more support for fund-seeking.

The importance of outreach work is underlined, particularly for women in rural areas, single parents, women from ethnic minorities, women returners and some Welsh-speaking women. Employing women with appropriate characteristics (including attention to ethnic origin) to do this is helpful.

Lack of childcare facilities is a major barrier to take-up of mainstream training. This affects the timing of courses, and the need to develop innovative distance learning and other flexible methods of providing education and training.

Confidence-building is essential, especially if women are seeking to move into male dominated areas of education, training or work.

Long-term guidance and counselling are vital. The EC has recognised this and is seeking to address it in planning for LEONARDO DA VINCI and SOCRATES.

Flexible systems are needed. Routes of progression need to be developed, with modular units available allowing credit accumulation and transfer, and more points of entry to education and training systems.

Many more women role models in FE/HE institutions are needed, as senior teachers, trainers and managers. Women-only training works especially in new technologies; opportunities need to be developed. The importance and effectiveness of collaborative working are demonstrated by many of these initiatives.

5.4   CONCLUSION

This section, together with **Realising Potential**, demonstrates the energies and commitment going into women's education and training projects. The important issue is to ensure adequate funding for such measures and to seek to mainstream the ideas which appear to be working well. Further research to evaluate these measures would be valuable.

6.   CONCLUSIONS AND RECOMMENDATIONS

6.1   INTRODUCTION

The position of women in education and training in Wales is poor, and considerably worse than it is for men, or for women in England. It is a constraining factor in the development of the Welsh economy. While the picture is complex, the main message from the review of research and the analysis of statistics is that *education and training systems are highly segregated by gender*, both vertically and horizontally. Men tend to receive job-related training and predominate in scientific and engineering courses that have direct labour market links. This is reflected in women's lower achievements in NTETs. Women are more often found in Access courses, and lower levels of FE and HE. Subject choices are highly gendered. Women's qualifications are frequently not translated into labour market opportunities.

A key issue here is that equal opportunities in the form of *equal access do not result in equal outcome*. Education and training systems on the whole, for example, do not take on board the impact of the career break on women's training needs. The drive for credentialism means that women returners face an increasingly difficult time reintegrating into the labour market unless provision for returners and routes of progression are improved. Their childcare responsibilities need to be accommodated. The skills of women workers, particularly part-time workers, are under-developed. Much existing provision is simply not in effect open to women. Education and training systems need to be far more flexible.

While there have been many excellent *initiatives,* started largely by women to provide women-friendly training, they are peripheral to mainstream provision and precariously funded. There are exemplary projects, illustrating innovative and effective forms of training: but they are only able to accommodate a fraction of those who need such training. It is essential to support these initiatives, but also to *mainstream* the good practices they have developed. This implies moving towards developing education and training systems which can accommodate the *diversity* of characteristics and circumstances of both women and men.

Wales has a particular set of institutions and social and economic characteristics which offer *challenges and opportunities*. The transfer of many responsibilities in education and training to Wales allows tailor-made policies to be developed. The policy context, and particularly the commitment to build a 'high quality, high-productivity economy', expressed in the Welsh Office document **People and Prosperity: A Challenge to Wales** (Welsh Office 1993b), provides a unique opportunity to put the issue of women's education and training needs, and the needs of the economy for the development of women's skills, high on the agenda. At the same time, as a low-wage, low-skill economy, with women predominating in part-time, low-skilled work, there is clearly a major task to be done in seizing the opportunity to develop policies which address this issue effectively. The dominance of small and medium-sized enterprises and the rural nature of much of the Principality creates difficulties for education and training provision. The highly gendered workforce and relatively low economic activity rates of women create a culture where women are not expected to be and are not found in top jobs. The issue here is to integrate policies on women's training needs with economic development policies more broadly.

A strength within Wales is the *partnership approach*, of which Chwarae Teg is a prime example. The work it has already done has helped to make training providers, employers and others aware of the need for more effective policies. It is a source of great strength in developing working relationships and raising awareness.

The fact that much of the population of Wales is based in areas with transport difficulties, such as the South Wales valleys or the rural areas implies that open and *distance learning* techniques would be particularly worthwhile investigating. Satellite technology enables the remotest areas to receive training in up-to-date technologies and skills. The European Union has been active in supporting such developments and transnational partnerships offer a way forward.

To achieve some of these goals, this final section of the report identifies research priorities, and policy implications for the education and training of women.

6.2   RESEARCH PRIORITIES

Gender issues in education and training can be usefully elaborated through many research avenues; here, we focus on those which are either especially current in the light of the many changes being experienced in these fields, or are related closely to the situation in Wales, as identified in this report.

We present these as a list of useful research areas rather than as an integrated package.

(i) The basis of education and training established in the immediate *post-compulsory years 16–18* is a vital one. The data show that young women stay on in education in significantly larger numbers than men, but far less is known about the nature and quality of the courses pursued, the problem of drop-out, and the reasons why men have 'caught up' so quickly at age 18. This warrants further investigation.

(ii) Especially in the light of the rapid and recent marketisation and transfer of responsibilities to Wales, a project is needed that would identify the *position of women in management of and decision-making in education and training organisations in Wales*. This would identify to what extent these organisations monitor the gender make-up of their own staff and assist in the development of strategies to develop equal opportunities awareness, training and polices within those key organisations. Examples of good practice from some can be offered as models to others. The organisations concerned are: the boards and senior staff of TECs, Welsh Office Industry and Training, WDA, FE and HE institutions and Funding Councils.

(iii) This report has shown how the volume of training in Wales is low, and the training participation of women in particular is weak. Sometimes this is 'explained' by the different economic structures from one area or region to another – size of firm, economic sector, incidence of part-time work. A comparative study would very usefully elucidate (a) the degree to which the low position of women in training in Wales is to be 'explained' in this way; and (b) what can be done, in the light of these findings, to increase significantly access to training by women in Wales.

(iv) Research is needed on the *qualitative* experience of education and training by women, so that lessons in good practice can be mainstreamed. It is also needed on post-compulsory experiences of women not in education, training or employment; on women in decision-making in Wales, and on the low rates of employer sponsored job-related training for women in Wales. A study which 'tracked' the progress of women through contrasted training programmes would assist in the evaluation of various aspects of provision, routes of progression, and guidance and counselling.

(v) The report shows that poor provision and take-up of courses for women through the medium of Welsh is an area that needs addressing.

(vi) A feasibility study which explored the scope of distance learning in meeting some of the training needs for women identified in this report, especially in new technologies, management and business skills, would be worthwhile.

(vii) Barriers to women taking up job-related training is also an important area. The statistics show that it is a problem, but specific reasons for this in different industries and sectors need to be elucidated.

6.3   GENERAL POLICY IMPLICATIONS

Gender is the most important determinant of who participates in and is funded for what kind of course. The main need is to *transform* mainstream education and training provision so that it meets the highly diverse needs of individuals, irrespective of gender, while mainstreaming good practice from the various women's training projects that have developed so successfully in Wales. This section identifies key areas for development and is aimed at three main audiences: education and training providers, employers, and funding bodies. However, many other organisations such as the EOC itself clearly also have a role to play in developing some of these specific proposals.

Policy implications for education and training providers

*   *Lifelong guidance and counselling* are essential. This is timely given the reorganisation of the careers service and the growing importance attached to guidance and counselling by the EC. This needs to address the stereotyped choices and low aspirations of schoolgirls, the needs of unemployed women and returners and the career development of employees. The potential for developing mentoring arrangements, networks and role models needs to be explored effectively given the desperate shortage of women in senior posts.

*   The need for *confidence-building and de-stereotyping* has been well documented, especially for women returners and women training in male dominated subject areas. This needs to be built into mainstream provision as appropriate. However, if education and training provision in male dominated areas were to be made more women-friendly or gender-neutral at the same time, there would be less need for women to have to deal with an uncomfortable environment. Curriculum reviews should address this.

- *Routes of progression* need to be developed. As the work place is so gendered, with few women finding their way to top jobs, it is vital that women, especially returners, progress to more advanced levels of education and training before rejoining the labour force. The area where women have made most progress is into the professions, where ports of entry are governed by qualifications. Too many women returners return to low-level work where they do not then have opportunities to develop their potential any further.

- Colleges need to develop their own *childcare facilities* in order to meet the needs of women with children and thus ensure their access to higher and further education. The examples of partnerships between employers and colleges assisted by Chwarae Teg to provide nurseries are well worth emulating more widely. Post-compulsory education and training provision more generally needs to take into account childcare needs. Given the increased competition and the ageing of the student population, providers may well increasingly need to calculate the cost to enrolment figures of *not* making such provision.

- *Providers* need to be much more aware of gender issues. Guidelines for education and training providers would be useful on how to monitor the gender dimension of their activities. EOC, the Welsh Office and the Funding Councils might usefully combine efforts to produce guidelines on monitoring systems and how to integrate their findings into strategic policy development. This point is elaborated upon in the section on statistics.

- Training women and families in *business start-up* is crucial to the economic regeneration of many parts of Wales. Women have shown a keen interest in business development but appropriate training has not been forthcoming. The development of modules in this area is vital.

Policy implications for employers

- Clearly there is much less *employer-sponsored training* for women than for men. Is this entirely because women are not in those technical and managerial posts which tend to be targeted for training? Is it that women are more likely to work in small and medium-sized enterprises which on the whole are less likely to offer training than larger employers? What are the criteria for selection for training? How compatible is it to combine job-related training with domestic commitments? It would be useful if employers could review the criteria by which they select staff for training opportunities and consider how domestic, work and training commitments can be accommodated creatively.

- *Consortia of small and medium-sized enterprises* may come together, as they do in Germany, to provide more job-related training and experience for their workers. The example of Welsh Water teaming up with smaller companies through Opportunity 2000 is a good example of how positive partnerships can benefit all. Consortia of employers providing childcare with assistance from Chwarae Teg again shows what can be done.

- Learning lessons from those employers who have sought to *develop an awareness of equality issues as a business aim* is vital. Opportunity 2000 are seeking to disseminate information on this. Many companies in Europe and the US are now convinced of the business arguments and have implemented polices accordingly. These ideas need to reach a much wider audience so that women who are trained do not then have their skills wasted. Employers' organisations can help in this dissemination.

- *Training for all employees* but particularly personnel officers, senior management and line managers is necessary to help the organisation to 'own' the goal of equality and recognise women's potential.

Policy implications for funding

- Given the increased focus on women's training in the EC, it is vital to ensure that applications for *ESF and Structural Funds* take advantage of the opportunities of securing funding for women's projects. Funds available from the EC have proved to be a lifeline to important initiatives in the field of women's education and training in Wales. Given its new focus on women's training, the EC as a source of funding will be of greater significance in the future and resources will need to be accessed more effectively. This is especially the case as the new Funding Councils cannot pay for the essential childcare facilities needed by so many women.

- There is a legacy of women who missed out on education first-time round, who will need their skills developed to participate in the workforce between now and the end of the century. Financial systems need to take this on board. In particular, cuts in *maintenance grants* should be avoided. It is essential that FEFCW and HEFCW ensure the maintenance of the level of access funds because they supplement the maintenance grants for women with particular needs, including childcare and other dependent needs.

• Women's *business networks* are effective in developing the confidence of new women entrepreneurs. They can supplement enterprise training and be used as a source of role models, mentors, speakers on courses and even loan guarantors. Such networks are developing in many parts of Wales and need financial support.

• *Training trainers* who can train women in, for example, new technologies but who also understand women's confidence problems, is vital. Women-only training workshops always have difficulty in recruiting suitably qualified women, and mainstream technology departments often have few women staff.

6.4   POLICY IMPLICATIONS ON STATISTICS AND GENDER MONITORING

There is a substantial volume of data and statistics already gathered across the different sectors in Wales which shed considerable light upon the gendering of post-school education and training. Some of this is published. A substantial proportion of it however remains unpublished, having been gathered for administrative purposes or as part of national surveys, only some of which is then analysed and released. One indication of the degree to which relevant statistics are gathered is the fact that this report is able to draw on existing sources: gender breakdowns are far more common in education and training statistics than those relating, say, to the Welsh language or disability.

Yet, the efforts required to prepare even this initial review in Wales demonstrate, however, that an accessible source based on those data that is comprehensive in coverage and comparable in methods of calculation, is not readily and publicly available to inform debate and policy development, despite the transfer of so many of these areas of responsibility to Wales. Even the data which are available distinguishing between men and women are frequently presented in such a form that the gender dimension is not transparent without undertaking substantial calculations. This occurs, for example, when detailed tables are published in 'raw' form, based on numbers of students, trainees, enrolments or qualifications so that patterns comparing men and women are obscured by sheer detail. Monitoring of the situation so that progress and problems can be followed, relating to both the different parts of education and training systems and the different geographical areas of Wales, calls for clear information measures. Indeed, it requires annual gender monitoring of participation, spend, qualifications, and so on. The indicators used must be valid and relevant to the full range of settings of education and training rather than be restricted to those aspects which happen to be the most 'data-rich'. In other words, gender monitoring should be built in to all key dimensions of post-compulsory education and training.

But while a great deal of information is already gathered in one form or another, this does not mean that the information base is adequate, leaving the main task only to present it in a more 'user-friendly' form. There is considerable variation in the ways that data are gathered, their scope and coverage, definitions used, and so on across the different organisations providing post-compulsory education and training and from one sector to another. Our contacts in preparation of this report, for instance, revealed substantial variations across Welsh colleges in the content and form of records kept, and still more from one TEC to another.

Some parts of the education and training systems are required to make statistical returns, often including breakdowns by gender, for administrative and funding purposes and in these cases, variations are reduced. Elsewhere, record-keeping is less consistent, with only patchy coverage of the gender dimension. But while we believe that it is very important that the database that will allow effective gender monitoring be improved, we are also mindful that it is easy to overwhelm education and training organisations with demands for data, distracting them from their main task of teaching and training. That is why it is especially important that reflection is given to precisely what information is needed, rather than just gathering it for its own sake. Moreover, it is essential that education and training providers themselves use the data to monitor their own performance at the institutional level, and build the results into strategic planning.

Building up the information base which will permit gender monitoring is thus partly a matter of using more effectively what is already gathered, at least by the exemplary education and training organisations. But it is a task which calls for much more than ensuring the accessible presentation and publication of statistics. It calls for the precise identification of the key elements that require monitoring. Current data from different sources in Wales then need to be assessed in order to identify outstanding gaps to be filled. It may be not so much that new data are required, but that existing data need standardising and topping up.

87

Improving information and data does not take place in the abstract, but is squarely located in the real world of institutions and agencies. This underlines the value of devoting attention to the mechanisms of data collection and management and to the context in which they take place, with regard to the degree to which this context facilitates or hinders better information flow. The marketisation trends discussed earlier might be expected to exacerbate variability in data collection, even to the point where some parts of the education and training system are able to downgrade the importance of data-gathering altogether (which would of course reduce still further the possibilities for all-Wales effective gender monitoring). On the basis of the evidence from our work, however, there seems to be a widespread and growing awareness of the need for better and more consistent information. This suggests there is a positive climate for the development of the data that will permit effective monitoring.

Two further specific issues warrant attention here. First, while we have stressed the value of collecting information to permit gender monitoring at the all-Wales level, and in the main sub-Wales areas (counties, districts, TEC areas and so on), there is also the crucial level of the individual organisation to consider. Monitoring should be integrated as a normal part of the planning process of schools, colleges enterprises, training providers, TECs, LEAs and so forth. This is not a matter separate from the more macro-level monitoring we have been discussing, for the indicators developed for system-wide use will also provide some of the benchmarks with which individual organisations can assess their progress. This is partly a matter of comparing the results generated at the local level with all-Wales and county averages. It is also a case of developing the tools at the national levels that permit individual organisations to monitor their performance and progress as regards the participation and representation of women and men in the different branches, programmes and levels of post-school education and training in Wales.

Second, there is a limitation inherent in some of the most interesting data gathered. Gender is rarely combined with other variables to allow insight into distribution patterns. Distribution by gender, ethnic origin and location may be presented, but this is rarely broken down further to see how gender interrelates with other dimensions. To address many questions, it is necessary to know how gender, age, previous qualifications and so on interrelate. The design and management of information systems can thus be scrutinised in order to see if they permit the generation of cross-tabulations.

From all these considerations, some main conclusions and recommendations emerge. Accurate, usable statistics are vital for gender monitoring. There is a need to ensure that those statistics that are published are presented in a form which allows the gender dimension – showing within and between gender differences – to emerge clearly. The consolidation of existing data-gathering, and the compilation of new statistics will be needed for gender monitoring to be effective across all the settings for education and training in Wales. This will call for consistency of methodology, standardisation of definition, and comparability of measures across Wales. All-Wales databases can prove very effective in promoting such an improvement. It is hoped that work currently being undertaken by the Welsh Education and Training Information Working Group will make a significant contribution.

To ensure that coverage is comprehensive, four aspects of indicator development will need to be to the fore. First, theoretical input is vital to ensure that adequate measures have been developed for the purpose. Second, standardisation of record-keeping across the counties and areas of Wales and across individual institutions will help overcome existing inconsistencies. Third, attention needs to be paid to the range of measures required – including consideration of such aspects as drop-out, destination, completion rates, and staffing – in addition to those of participation and enrolment. Fourth, areas where data tend to be weak, as is the case for many aspects of enterprise training, must become priorities so that the reviews of the situation of women and education and training in Wales are not partial.

In order that data collection is effective and yet not excessively burdensome, the collaborative development of an agreed set of indicators would be most useful. This would also help to identify what gaps exist. On this basis, a 'gender scorecard' for education and training providers could be produced on a regular basis in an accessible form for a variety of audiences, both professional and the public at large.

The process of indicator development and the production of a 'gender scorecard' would also assist in the generation of guidelines for gender monitoring which could be used in a number of different settings in education and training. The results of the scorecard would also provide benchmarks against which the experience of individual organisations and institutions can be compared.

Establishing gender monitoring systems is, however, just a first step in seeking to open up education and training to women. The next step is to use the data generated, at an individual institution and at wider aggregate levels to develop effective strategies. For this purpose, guidelines on using such data in strategic planning would be helpful.

6.5   CONCLUSION

Mainstreaming good practice from the many excellent initiatives in women's education and training in Wales must be the long-term goal. This includes attention to childcare, flexibility, modularisation, guidance and counselling, family-friendly hours, confidence-building, affordable fees, routes of progression, women-only training where appropriate, distance learning and so on. Developing the economy of Wales relies particularly upon developing the skills of women, but it will take a concerted effort by a considerable number of individuals and organisations to develop statistics and monitoring systems, and transform the culture of post-compulsory education and training in Wales to facilitate women to develop their skills to their full potential.

BIBLIOGRAPHY

Aaron, J. and Rees, T. (1994) 'Identities in Transition' *in* Aaron, J., Rees, T., Betts, S. and Vincentelli, M. (eds.) **Our Sisters' Land: The Changing Identities of Women in Wales**. Cardiff: University of Wales Press.

Allen, S. and Truman, C. (eds.) (1993) **Women in Business: Perspectives on Women Entrepreneurs**. London: Routledge.

Ashton, S. (1994) 'The Farmer Needs a Wife: Farm Workers in Wales' *in* Aaron, J., Rees, T., Betts, S. and Vincentelli, M. (eds.) **Our Sisters' Land: The Changing Identities of Women in Wales**. Cardiff: University of Wales Press.

Beddoe, D. (1986) 'Images of Welsh Women' *in* Curtis, T. (ed.) **Wales: The Imagined Nation**. Bridgend: Poetry Wales Press, pp. 227–38.

Bellin, W., Osmond, J. and Reynolds, D. (1994) **Towards an Educational Policy for All.** Cardiff: Institute of Welsh Affairs.

Betts, S. (1994) 'The Changing Family in Wales' *in* Aaron, J., Rees, T., Betts, S. and Vincentelli, M. (eds.) **Our Sisters' Land: The Changing Identities of Women in Wales**. Cardiff: University of Wales Press.

Career Development Loans (1993) **Annual Report 1992–1993**. London: Department of Employment.

Careers Service in Wales (1994) **Pupil Destination Statistics in Wales, 1993,** in co-operation with BP Chemicals Ltd. Cardiff: Careers Service in Wales.

Central Statistical Office (1993) **Regional Trends 28**. London: HMSO.

Chwarae Teg (1993a) **An Audit of Childcare in Wales**. Pontypridd: Chwarae Teg.

Chwarae Teg (1993b) **Good Childcare, Better Business: A Guide to Childcare Initiatives in Wales**. Pontypridd: Chwarae Teg.

Clarke, K. (1991) **Women and Training: A Review,** EOC Research Discussion Series**, no. 1,** Manchester: Equal Opportunities Commission.

Coleman, S. (1994) 'Doing it for Themselves', **Western Mail,** Tuesday 26 April, p. 7.

Commission of the European Communities (1993a) **Growth, Competitiveness, Employment: The Challenges and Ways Forward into the 21st Century,** White Paper. Luxembourg: Office for Official Publications of the European Communities.

Commission of the European Communities (1993b) **European Social Policy: Options for the Future,** Green Paper. Luxembourg: Office for Official Publications of the European Communities.

Commission of the European Communities (1993c) **Social Partners' Joint Opinion on Women and Training.** Brussels: Commission of the European Communities.

Commission of the European Communities (1993d) **EC Education and Training Programmes 1986–92. Results and Achievements: An Overview.** Brussels: Commission of the European Communities.

Daniel, P. (1994) 'Promoting Gender Equality in Schools' *in* Aaron, J., Rees, T., Betts, S. and Vincentelli, M. (eds.) **Our Sisters' Land: The Changing Identities of Women in Wales.** Cardiff: University of Wales Press.

Department for Education (1993) **Statistical Bulletin on Women in Post-compulsory Education,** Issue 26/93, December. London: Department for Education.

Department of Education and Science, Department of the Environment, Welsh Office (1991) **Education and Training for the 21st Century, Volume One,** White Paper presented to Parliament, May. London: HMSO.

Department of Employment (1993a) **Training Statistics 1993**. London: HMSO.

Department of Employment (1993b) **New Earnings Survey 1993, Part E.** London: HMSO.

Equal Opportunities Commission (1993) **Formal Investigation into the Publicly Funded Vocational Training System in England and Wales.** Manchester: Equal Opportunities Commission.

Equal Opportunities Commission/Chwarae Teg (1993) **Realising Potential: Increasing the Effectiveness of Education and Training Provision for Women.** Cardiff: Equal Opportunities Commission.

ERES (1994) **A Study of the Economically Inactive and Their Role in the Labour Market,** Report for the Welsh Office Statistics and Economics Divisions. Cardiff: ERES.

Essex, S., Callender, C., Rees, T. and Winckler, V. (1986) **New Styles of Training for Women: An Evaluation of South Glamorgan Women's Workshop.** Manchester: Equal Opportunities Commission.

Fielder, S. and Rees, T. (1991) **Telecoms and Telecommunications: Report to South Glamorgan Women's Workshop.** Cardiff: Social Research Unit, University of Wales College of Cardiff.

Francis, M. and Pudner, H. (1994) 'Women in the Workforce: Alternative Choices for Women from Coalmining Areas – Partnerships in Community Development', **Equal Opportunities International,** vol. 13, no. 3/4/5, pp. 50–61.

Garland, P. (1992) **North Wales Access Consortium Research Project.** Bangor: University College of North Wales Bangor.

Garland, P. (1994) 'Educating Rhian: Experiences of Mature Women Students in North Wales' *in* Aaron, J., Rees, T., Betts, S. and Vincentelli, M. (eds.) **Our Sisters' Land: The Changing Identities of Women in Wales.** Cardiff: University of Wales Press.

Gateway Europe (1993a) **Women Entrepreneurs, Skills Training and Enterprise Development,** Report for Commission of the European Communities Task Force Human Resources Education Training and Youth.

Gateway Europe (1993b) **Synthesis Report of the Athena Project.** Pontypridd: Gateway Europe.

Gateway Europe (1993c) **Training for Development in Europe**. Pontypridd: Gateway Europe.

Gateway Europe (1993d) **Directory of Welsh Involvement in European Education, Training and Youth Programmes.** Pontypridd: Gateway Europe/Welsh Development Agency.

Griffiths, M. (1992) **North Wales Access to Higher Education Students: Who are they? Where are 'the Cymry'?** Wales Access Unit/North Wales Access Consortium.

Gwent TEC (1993) **Labour Market Assessment 1992/3**. Newport: Gwent TEC.

Hansard Society Commission on Women at the Top (1990) **Report of the Hansard Society Commission on Women at the Top.** London: Hansard Society.

Institute of Welsh Affairs (1994) **Towards an Educational Policy for Wales.** Cardiff: Institute of Welsh Affairs.

Istance, D., Rees, G. and Williamson, H. (1994) **Young People not in Education, Training or Employment in South Glamorgan.** Cardiff: South Glamorgan TEC.

Jones, H. M. (1993) 'A Survey of the Welsh Language: The 1992 Welsh Social Survey', **Statistical News,** vol. 102. London: HMSO.

Lane, N. (1994) **The Rising Tide: A Report on Women in Science, Engineering and Technology**. London: HMSO.

Le Grand, J. and Bartlett, W. (eds.) (1993) **Quasi-markets and Social Policy**. London: Macmillan.

Lloyd, C. (1992) 'Tailor-made Occupations: A Study of Gender and Skill in the Welsh Clothing Industry', **Contemporary Wales: An Annual Review of Economic and Social Research**, vol. 5, pp. 115–30.

Lodge, P., Parry-Langdon, N., Fielder, S. (1991) **The Experience of Access Course Students Proceeding to Selected Higher Education Institutions in Wales**. Cardiff: Wales Access Unit and School of Social and Administrative Studies, University of Wales, Cardiff.

MacNamara, F. (1990) 'Women and Training', University of Wales College of Cardiff MSc Econ in Women's Studies, unpublished dissertation.

Malvisi, J., Robinson, P. and Willox, I. (1990) **Expanding the Role of Women in the South Wales Workforce.** Cardiff: Welsh Development Agency.

Metcalf, H. and Leighton, P. (1989) **The Under-utilisation of Women in the Labour Market.** IMS Report for the Equal Opportunities Commission, no. 172. Brighton: Institute of Manpower Studies.

Morris, D. (1994) 'Comparative Study of Language, Gender and the Labour Market: Wales, Friesland and Galicia'. Bangor: University College of North Wales.

National Advisory Council for Education and Training Targets (1994) **Report on Progress,** London: NACETT.

New, J. (1991) 'Access Courses Suitable for Women', University of Wales College of Cardiff MEd, unpublished dissertation.

North West Regional Research Laboratory (1993) **Economic Activity in TEC Areas of Wales: An Analysis of 1991 Census Data,** Report to Welsh Office. Lancaster: Lancaster University.

Office of Her Majesty's Chief Inspector of Schools in Wales (1994) **Review of Educational Provision in Wales 1992–3**. London: HMSO.

Office of Population, Censuses and Surveys (OPCS) (1994) **1991 Census: Wales**. London: HMSO.

Owen, D. (1994) **Black and Ethnic Minority Women and the Labour Market.** Manchester: Equal Opportunities Commission.

Pilcher, J., Delamont, S., Powell, G. and Rees, T. (1988) 'The Women's Training Roadshow and the "Manipulation" of Schoolgirls' Career Choices', **British Journal of Education and Work,** vol. 2, no. 2, pp. 61–66.

Pilcher, J., Delamont, S., Powell, G., Rees, T. and Read, M. (1989a) 'Evaluating a Careers Convention: Methods, Results and Implications', **Research Papers in Education**, vol. 4, no. 1, pp. 57–76.

Pilcher, J., Delamont, S., Powell, G., Rees, T. and Read, M. (1989b) 'Challenging Occupational Stereotypes: Women's Training Roadshows and Guidance at School Level', **British Journal of Guidance and Counselling**, vol .17, no. 1, pp. 59–67.

Pilcher, J., Delamont, S., Powell, G., Rees, T. and Read, M. (1990) **An Evaluative Study of Cardiff Women's Training Roadshow.** Cardiff: Welsh Office.

Rees, C. and Willox, I. (1991a) **Expanding the Role of Women in the South Wales Workforce.** Cardiff: Welsh Development Agency.

Rees, C. and Willox, I. (1991b) 'A Survey of Women's Experiences and Perceptions of the South Wales Labour Market'. Research programme on Expanding the Role of Women in the South Wales Workforce. Cardiff: Welsh Development Agency

Rees, G. and Fielder, S. (1992) 'The Services Economy, Sub-contracting and New Employment Relations: Contract Catering and Cleaning', **Work, Employment and Society,** vol. 6, no. 2, pp. 347–68.

Rees, G. and Rees, T. (1980) 'Education Inequality in Wales: Some Problems and Paradoxes' *in* Rees, G. and Rees, T.L. (eds.) **Poverty and Social Inequality in Wales**. London: Croom Helm, pp. 71–92.

Rees, G., Fielder, S. and Rees, T. (1991) 'Training Needs and Provision: The Bridgend Case Study', Institutional Determinants of Adult Training, End of Award Report to ESRC (Grant No. XC1125009). Cardiff: School of Social and Administrative Studies, University of Wales College of Cardiff.

Rees, G., Winckler, V. and Williamson, H. (1990) **Employers' Recruitment Strategies, Vocational Education and Training: An Analysis of a Loose Labour Market**. Cardiff: School of Social and Administrative Studies, University of Wales College of Cardiff.

Rees, G., Rees, T., Fielder, S. and Parry-Langdon, N. (1989) **The Supply of and Demand for Low Level IT Skills in Mid and South Glamorgan**. Cardiff: Social Research Unit, University of Wales College of Cardiff.

Rees, G., Tweedale, I., Rees, T. and Read, M. (1988) 'Adult Training Policy and Local Labour Markets', **British Journal of Education and Work**, vol. 2, no. 1, pp. 1–16.

Rees, T. (1988) 'Changing Patterns of Women's Work in Wales: Some Myths Explored', **Contemporary Wales**, vol. 2, pp. 119–30. Cardiff: University of Wales Press.

Rees, T. (1989) 'Meeting the Labour Shortage – Women and Training into the 1990s', **Labour Market Wales**, no. 2, pp. 2–3.

Rees, T. (1992) **Women and the Labour Market**. London: Routledge.

Rees, T. (1993a) **Women and the EC Training Programmes,** Report to the Commission of the European Communities. Bristol: School for Advanced Urban Studies, University of Bristol.

Rees, T. (1993b) 'Women's Training Workshops in New Information Technologies', **International Journal of Community Education**, vol. 1, no. 4, pp. 22–25.

Rees, T. (1994a) 'Women and Paid Work' *in* Aaron, J., Rees, T., Betts, S. and Vincentelli, M. (eds.) **Our Sisters' Land: The Changing Identities of Women in Wales**. Cardiff: University of Wales Press.

Rees, T. (1994b) 'Information Technology Skills and Access to Training Opportunities: Germany and the UK' *in* Ducatel, K. (ed.) **Employment and Technical Change in Europe: Work Organization, Skills and Training**. London: Edward Arnold.

Rees, T. (1994c) **Athena: Skills, Training and Women's Economic Development.** Report of a Conference held in Ewloe, North Wales. Pontypridd: Gateway Europe/Welsh Development Agency.

Rees, T. (1994d) 'Feminising the Mainstream: Women and the EC Training Programmes', **Equal Opportunities International,** vol. 13, no. 3/4/5, pp. 9–28.

Rees, T. and Fielder, S. (1991) **Women and Top Jobs in Wales,** Report for HTV Wales Cardiff. Social Research Unit, University of Wales College of Cardiff.

Rees, T. and Fielder, S. (1992) 'Through the Dark Glass Ceiling: Women and Top Jobs in Wales' *in* **Contemporary Wales: An Annual Review of Economic and Social Research,** vol. 5, pp. 99–114.

Rees, T. and Winckler, V. (1986) 'Last Hired, First Fired?' **Planet: The Welsh Internationalist,** no. 57, pp. 38–41.

Rees, T., Williamson, H. and Harris, A. (eds.) (1990) **Welsh Journal of Education – Special Issue on Enterprise Education,** vol. 1, no. 2.

Road, A. (1994) 'Mining New Wisdom: A Prefab University has Brought Fresh Hope to a Depressed Welsh Valley', **Observer,** 23 January.

Salisbury, J. (1994) 'Chasing Credentials: Women Further Education Teachers and In-service Training' *in* Aaron, J., Rees, T., Betts, S. and Vincentelli, M. (eds.) **Our Sisters' Land: The Changing Identities of Women in Wales**. Cardiff: University of Wales Press.

Slade, R. and Yates, J. (eds.) (1993) **School Leavers Destinations 1992**, ACC/AMA/UK Heads of Careers Service.

Smith, I. (1993) 'How Learned is my Valley: A Community University is Soon to Open in Welsh Mining Country' **The Times,** 27 September.

Thomas, D. (1992) 'Wales in 1990: An Economic Survey' *in* **Contemporary Wales: An Annual Review of Economic and Social Research**, vol. 5, pp. 213–64.

Training Agency (1989) **Training in Britain: A Study of Funding, Activity and Attitudes – The Main Report.** London: HMSO.

University Statistical Record (1993) **University Statistics 1992–93, Volume One: Students and Staff**. Cheltenham: USR.

Venus, J. (1993) 'Chwarae Teg (Fair Play) Evaluation and Feasibility Study Report'. Pontypridd: Chwarae Teg.

Wales Access Unit (1993) **Access Provision in Wales 1988/89 – 1992/93**. Cardiff: Wales Access Unit.

Wales TUC (1994a) **Annual Report,** Cardiff: Wales TUC.

Wales TUC (1994b) **Tackling the Low Pay, No Jobs Economy**. Cardiff: Wales TUC.

Welsh Development Agency (1992) **Directory of Welsh Involvement in European Community Education, Training and Youth Programmes.** Pontypridd: Welsh Development Agency.

Welsh Office (1992) **Statistics of Education in Wales: Schools, No. 5 1991**. Cardiff: Welsh Office.

Welsh Office (1993a) **Further and Higher Education and Training Statistics in Wales, No. 1, 1993.** Cardiff: Government Statistical Service.

Welsh Office (1993b) **People and Prosperity: A Challenge to Wales** Cardiff: Welsh Office.

Welsh Office (1994a) **Further and Higher Education and Training Statistics in Wales, No.2, 1994.** Cardiff: Government Statistical Service.

Welsh Office (1994b) **Welsh Economic Trends.** Cardiff: Welsh Office.

Welsh Office (1994c) **Statistics of Education and Training in Wales: Schools, No. 2, 1994.** Cardiff: Welsh Office.

Willox, I. (1992) **Under-utilisation of Skills in North West Wales.** Pontypridd: Welsh Development Agency.

Willox, I. and Virgin, K. (1991) **The Provision of Education and Training for Women,** carried out as part of the research programme 'Expanding the Role of Women in the South Wales Workforce'. Pontypridd: Welsh Development Agency.

Willox, I. and Virgin, K. (1992) **The Provision of Education and Training for Women,** carried out as part of the research programme 'Expanding the Role of Women in North and Rural Wales Workforce'. Pontypridd: Welsh Development Agency.

APPENDIX I.   LIST OF ORGANISATIONS CONTACTED

Assembly of Welsh Counties

Chwarae Teg

Commission of the European Union Task Force

    Human Resources Education Training and Youth

Department of Employment, Career Development Loans

Dove Workshop, Banwen

Equal Opportunities Commission

Further Education Colleges (all)

Further Education Funding Council

Further Education Unit in Wales

Gateway Europe

Higher Education Funding Council for Wales

Open University in Wales

Powys County Council

Project Grace

South Glamorgan Women's Workshop, Cardiff

Training and Enterprise Councils (7)

University of Glamorgan

University College Swansea

University Statistical Record

Valleys Women's Roadshow

Wales Access Unit

Wales Co-operative Centre

Wales TUC

Welsh Office, Statistics Department

Welsh Office Training, Education and Enterprise Department

APPENDIX II. MEMBERS OF THE PROJECT STEERING AND ADVISORY GROUP

Ms Pat Bayliss	Gwent TEC
Ms Swinder Chadha	Department of Continuing Education, University of Wales, Cardiff
Ms Val Feld	EOC
Ms Jane Hutt	Chwarae Teg
Dr David Perfect	EOC
Ms Sheila Pickard	FEFCW
Ms Anne Poole	NIACE Cymru
Mr John Sharman	EOC

APPENDIX III.   ADDITIONAL STATISTICAL TABLES

This appendix contains an additional set of tables to those contained in Chapter 4 (these are referred to by the prefix 'A'), which would otherwise encumber the text. They refer to patterns and trends in education and training where all-Wales figures are available. Where possible, both row and column distributions have been calculated. The row percentages (indicated by R in the tables) give the primary measure of gender patterns: they are *measures of equality or inequality of numbers between men and women*. Exact equality of numbers gives a 50/50 split; this compares with cases of a much more uneven division between men and women. The column percentages (C) represent a very useful complement to these basic measures of between-gender (in)equality by looking instead at within-gender patterns. That is, they show how women, on the one hand, and men, on the other, are distributed across, for instance, the different types of course or subjects at a given level. As such they are measures of the concentration of men and women across the different categories in question.

A1   Recent trends in main destinations of pupils attaining the minimum school-leaving age, by gender, 1989–93

A2   Trends in full-time equivalent course enrolments in maintained and grant-aided establishments of further and non-university higher education, by gender, 1987/88 –1991/92

A3   Trends in students and gender distributions in further education, by mode of attendance, 1987/88, 1989/90, 1992/93 (November)

A4   Trends in enrolments on further education courses at maintained and grant-aided major establishments in Wales, by gender and qualification, 1987/88, 1990/91, 1992/93 (November)

A5   Trends in students and gender distributions in non-university higher education in Wales, by mode of attendance, 1987/88, 1989/90, 1992/93 (November)

A6   Enrolments in non-university higher education courses, by subject of study and gender, 1992/93 (November)

A7   Trends in enrolments in full-time courses of initial teacher training, by course and gender, 1987/88, 1989/90, 1991/92

A8   First-year students enrolled on full-time courses of initial teacher training, by age and gender, 1991/92

A9   Welsh undergraduates at universities in the United Kingdom on full-time or sandwich courses, by subject group and gender, 1992/93 (December)

A10   Proportions of Welsh undergraduates to all UK undergraduates and percentage differences from same-sex averages, 1991/92

A11   Welsh postgraduates at university in the United Kingdom, by subject group and gender, 1992/93 (December)

A12   Proportions of Welsh postgraduates to all UK postgraduates and percentage differences from same-sex averages, 1991/92

A13   Open University undergraduate students in Wales, course registration, by faculty and gender, 1990 to 1992

A14   Open University undergraduates, by gender, age, and whether new/continuing, 1992

A15   Full-time teachers in non-university higher and further education, by gender and grade, 1990 and 1992

A16   Full-time university staff, by grade and gender, University of Wales and GB, 1992 (31 December)

A17   Enrolments at LEA adult education centres, by mode of study and gender, 1991/92

Table A1 Recent trends in main destinations of pupils attaining the minimum school-leaving age, by gender, 1989–93

Main destination	Total N	1989 F C(%) R(%)	M C(%) R(%)	Total N	1991 F C(%) R(%)	M C(%) R(%)	Total N	1993 F C(%) R(%)	M C(%) R(%)
Education	19,784	59.9 56.4	44.7 43.6	21,792	69.2 53.8	56.0 46.2	22,049	74.9 52.1	64.8 47.9
YT	9,380	19.6 38.9	29.7 61.1	5,565	11.7 35.7	19.9 64.3	3,701	7.6 31.7	15.5 68.3
Employment:	4,470	10.4 43.4	14.7 56.6	2,875	6.5 38.0	9.9 62.0	2,004	5.6 43.0	7.0 57.0
(with planned training)	(1,687)	(3.0) 33.1	(5.9) 66.9	(111)	(2.0) 30.0	(4.3) 70.0	(683)	(1.8) 41.0	(2.5) 59.0
(no planned training)	(3,083)	(7.4) 44.8	(8.8) 55.2	(1,764)	(4.5) 43.1	(5.6) 56.9	(1,321)	(3.8) 44.0	(4.5) 56.0
Known but in none of above	1,961	5.0 47.0	5.4 53.0	2,715	6.9 43.0	8.6 57.0	2,530	7.8 47.4	8.2 52.6
Missing	2,003	5.1 47.3	5.5 52.7	1,953	5.7 49.3	5.5 50.7	1,354	4.1 46.1	4.5 53.9
TOTAL	37,898	100 49.1	100 50.9	34,900	100 48.5	100 51.5	31,638	100 48.5	100 51.5

Note: C = column, R = row.

Source: Careers Services in Wales (1994) pp. 2–3.

Table A2 Trends in full-time equivalent course enrolments in maintained and grant-aided establishments of further and non-university higher education, by gender, 1987/88–1991/92

	Non-university higher education course enrolments			Further education course enrolments		
	N	F(%)	M(%)	N	F(%)	M(%)
1987/88	14,893	43.4	56.6	29,805	50.6	49.4
1988/89	15,480	44.4	55.6	30,889	50.4	49.6
1989/90	16,258	44.8	55.2	32,611	50.8	49.2
1990/91	17,638	46.9	53.1	34,486	51.5	48.5
1991/92	21,049	47.7	52.3	38,606	51.8	48.2

Source: Welsh Office (1993a) Table 2.03.

Table A3 **Trends in students and gender distributions in further education, by mode of attendance, 1987/88, 1989/90, 1992/93 (November)**

Mode of attendance	1987/88 Total	F C(%) R(%)	M C(%) R(%)	1989/90 Total	F C(%) R(%)	M C(%) R(%)	1992/93[3] Total	F C(% R(%)	M C(%) R(%)
Full-time[1]	19,750	31.7 57.7	24.6 42.3	21,608	30.6 57.8	24.0 42.2	30,825	33.8 53.6	35.0 46.4
Sandwich	2,087	0.7 12.5	5.4 87.5	1,674	0.5 11.2	3.9 88.8	991	0.3 16.3	2.0 83.7
Part-time day:	24,597	25.1 36.7	45.9 63.3	27,126	23.9 35.9	45.8 64.1	25,643	24.3 46.3	33.8 53.7
– Day and block release	(18,539)	(15.9) 30.8	(37.8) 69.2	(21,241)	(14.5) 27.8	(40.3) 72.2	(15,604)	(10.7) 33.5	(25.4) 66.5
– Not released	(6,058)	(9.2) 54.7	(8.1) 45.3	(5,885)	(9.4) 65.1	(5.4) 34.9	(10,039)	(13.6) 66.1	(8.3) 33.9
Other [2]	23,403	42.4 65.1	24.1 34.9	28,405	45.1 64.7	26.4 35.3	32,229	41.6 63.0	29.2 37.0
TOTAL	69,837	100 51.4	100 48.6	78,813	100 51.8	100 48.2	89,688	100 54.5	100 45.5

Notes: [1] Includes short full-time and short course.
[2] Includes evening only, open and distance learning.
[3] Excludes 6th-form colleges.
C = column, R = row.

Source: Welsh Office (1993a) Table 3.02, plus data supplied by the Welsh Office.

Table A4   Trends in enrolments on further education courses at maintained and grant-aided major establishments in Wales, by gender and qualification, 1987/88, 1990/91, 1992/93 (November)

Qualification	1987/88 Total	1987/88 F C(%) R(%)	1987/88 M C(%) R(%)	1990/91 Total	1990/91 F C(%) R(%)	1990/91 M C(%) R(%)	1992/93[1] Total	1992/93 F C(%) R(%)	1992/93 M C(%) R(%)
In-service teacher training	50	0.1 / 62.0	0.1 / 38.0	–	– / –	– / –	–	– / –	– / –
BTEC Diploma	7,229	7.4 / 39.1	12.4 / 60.9	10,667	11.1 / 47.6	13.9 / 52.4	14,973	13.0 / 45.8	18.8 / 54.2
BTEC Certificate[2]	5,681	4.7 / 32.1	10.9 / 67.9	5,892	4.0 / 31.0	10.1 / 69.0	5,310	3.1 / 31.0	8.5 / 69.0
City and Guilds/Regional Examining Boards	17,920	15.6 / 33.5	33.5 / 66.5	19,002	10.9 / 26.3	35.0 / 73.7	17,437	9.9 / 29.8	28.3 / 70.2
Professional qualifications	8,014	16.9 / 81.0	4.3 / 19.0	12,068	22.1 / 83.8	4.9 / 16.2	13,791	21.6 / 82.4	5.6 / 17.6
'A'/'AS' levels	8,206	12.4 / 58.2	9.6 / 41.8	9,266	12.4 / 61.4	8.9 / 38.6	10,433	11.8 / 59.5	9.8 / 40.5
GCSE	9,221	15.5 / 64.6	9.2 / 35.4	10,333	15.4 / 68.3	8.2 / 31.7	11,295	14.2 / 66.4	8.8 / 33.6
Other specified qualifications	1,333	2.1 / 60.6	1.5 / 39.4	1,336	1.6 / 55.1	1.5 / 44.9	1,715	1.7 / 53.5	1.8 / 46.5
Schedule 2 courses	–	–	–	–	–	–	1,370	1.8 / 68.1	1.0 / 31.9
Unspecified qualifications	16,288	25.2 / 59.4	18.6 / 40.6	17,191	22.3 / 9.4	7.4 / 40.6	19,610	22.9 / 61.5	17.5 / 38.5
TOTAL	73,942	100 / 51.9	100 / 48.1	85,755	100 / 3.3	100 / 46.7	95,934	100 / 54.9	100 / 45.1

Notes: [1] 1992/93: excludes 6th-form colleges.
[2] 1992/93 figures include BTEC, NVQs and other BTECS.
C = column, R = row.

Source: Welsh Office (1993a) Table 2.08 and data supplied by Welsh Office (provisional when supplied, pending publication).

Table A5   Trends in students and gender distributions in non-university higher education in Wales, by mode of attendance, 1987/88, 1989/90, 1992/93 (November)

Mode of attendance	1987/88 Total	1989/90 F C(%) R(%)	1989/90 M C(%) R(%)	1989/90 Total	1992/93 F C(%) R(%)	1992/93 M C(%) R(%)	1992/93 Total	F C(%) R(%)	M C(%) R(%)
Full-time[1]	9,067	56.1 / 51.7	40.0 / 48.3	9,671	53.7 / 53.4	35.1 / 46.6	17,617	60.7 / 53.5	46.9 / 46.5
Sandwich	3,402	10.9 / 26.9	21.0 / 73.1	3,686	10.8 / 28.3	20.6 / 71.7	4,582	10.2 / 34.5	17.2 / 65.5
Part-time day:	5,946	23.9 / 33.5	33.3 / 66.5	111	25.9 / 35.0	36.0 / 65.0	8,932	22.9 / 39.9	30.7 / 60.1
– Day and block	(5,200)	(20.1) / 32.4	(29.7) / 67.6	(6,406)	(22.2) / 33.3	(33.3) / 66.7	(7,486)	(18.2) / 37.7	(26.7) / 62.3
– Not released	(746)	(3.7) / 41.7	(3.7) / 58.3	(705)	(3.7) / 50.2	(2.7) / 49.8	(1,446)	(4.8) / 51.1	(4.0) / 48.9
Other [2]	1,792	9.1 / 42.4	8.7 / 57.6	1,987	9.5 / 46.1	8.3 / 53.9	1,874	6.2 / 51.7	5.2 / 48.3
TOTAL	20,207	100 / 41.3	100 / 58.7	22,455	100 / 42.8	100 / 57.2	33,005	100 / 47.1	100 / 52.9

Notes: [1] includes short full-time and short course.
[2] includes evening only, open and distance learning.
C = column, R = row.

Source: Welsh Office (1993a) Table 3.02, plus data supplied by the Welsh Office (provisional pending publication when supplied).

Table A6   Enrolments in non-university higher education courses, by subject of study and gender, 1992/93 (November)

Subject	F C(%)	F R(%)	M C(%)	M R(%)	Total N	Total C(%)
Education	25.2	75.6	7.2	24.3	5,170	15.6
Medicine and dentistry	0.1	53.6	0.1	46.4	28	0.1
Other medical	5.8	79.5	1.3	20.5	1,141	3.4
Biological sciences	1.0	57.8	0.6	42.2	263	0.8
Agriculture and related	1.4	48.4	1.3	51.6	442	1.3
Physical sciences	2.0	42.3	2.4	57.7	742	2.2
Mathematics/computing	2.8	20.1	10.0	79.9	2,191	6.6
Engineering/technology	1.8	6.2	24.7	93.8	4,614	13.9
Architecture, building, planning	1.1	10.5	7.8	89.5	1,562	4.7
Social studies	11.2	63.3	5.7	36.7	2,742	8.3
Business/administration	28.9	50.9	24.7	49.1	8,824	26.7
Mass communication	1.3	59.1	0.8	40.9	342	1.0
Languages	0.5	82.1	0.1	17.9	95	0.3
Humanities	0.2	68.9	0.1	31.1	45	0.1
Creative arts, design	8.8	48.6	8.2	51.4	2,802	8.5
Combined and general	8.0	59.9	4.8	40.1	2,082	6.3
TOTAL	100 (15,545)	47.0	100 (17,540)	53.0	33,085	100

Note: C = column, R = row.

Source: Data supplied by the Welsh Office (provisional pending publication when supplied).

Table A7 Trends in enrolments in full-time courses of initial teacher training, by course and gender, 1987/88, 1989/90, 1991/92

Type of course	1987/88			1989/90			1991/92		
	N	F C(%) R(%)	M C(%) R(%)	N	F C(%) R(%)	M C(%) R(%)	N	F C(%) R(%)	M C(%) R(%)
Postgraduate Certificate of Education (PGCE)	915	24.7 59.1	42.6 40.9	918	23.7 60.7	43.0 39.3	1,126	21.9 59.8	41.8 40.2
BEd	1,569	57.3 79.9	35.9 20.1	2,270	76.3 78.9	57.0 21.1	3,033	78.1 79.2	58.2 20.8
DipHE	583	18.0 67.6	21.5 32.4	–	– –	– –	–	– –	– –
TOTAL	3,067	100 71.4	100 28.6	3,188	100 73.7	100 26.3	4,159	100 74.0	100 26.0
		(2,189)	(878)		(2,349)	(839)		(3,076)	(1,083)

Note: C = column, R = row.

Source: Welsh Office (1993a) Table 6.01.

110

Table A8 **First-year students enrolled on full-time courses of initial teacher training, by age and gender, 1991/92**

Age	Total	F C(%) R(%)	M C(%) R(%)	Total	F C(%) R(%)	M C(%) R(%)	Total	F C(% R(%)	M C(%) R(%)
18	376	29.5 88.6	11.9 11.4	–	– –	– –	376	21.4 88.6	6.2 11.4
19	239	17.2 81.2	12.4 18.8	–	– –	– –	239	12.5 81.2	6.5 18.8
20	74	5.3 81.2	3.9 18.8	4	0.5 50.0	0.6 50.0	78	4.0 79.5	2.3 20.5
21	123	8.3 76.4	8.0 23.6	145	22.8 66.9	14.5 33.1	268	12.3 71.3	11.1 28.7
22	99	6.7 75.8	6.6 24.2	146	23.2 67.8	14.2 32.2	245	11.2 71.0	10.2 29.0
23	60	3.6 68.3	5.2 31.7	83	11.3 57.8	10.5 42.2	143	5.7 62.2	7.8 37.8
24	48	2.8 66.7	4.4 33.3	58	8.0 58.6	7.2 41.4	106	4.2 62.3	5.8 37.7
25–29	175	9.6 61.7	18.5 38.3	176	17.4 42.0	30.7 58.0	351	11.7 51.9	24.4 48.1
30+	293	16.7 64.2	29.0 35.8	146	16.9 49.3	22.3 50.7	439	16.7 59.2	25.8 40.8
TOTAL	1,489[1]	100 75.7	100 24.3	758[1]	100 56.2	100 43.8	2,247[1]	100 69.1	100 30.9

Note: [1] includes age unknown.
C = column, R = row.

Source: Welsh Office (1993a) Table 6.05.

Table A9   Welsh undergraduates at universities in the United Kingdom on full-time or sandwich courses, by subject group and gender, 1992/93 (December)

Subject group	Female			Male			Total		
	N	C(%)	R(%)	N	C(%)	R(%)	N	C(%)	R(%)
Education	201	2.5	82.7	42	0.5	17.3	243	1.5	100
Medicine and health	1,787	22.0	67.8	849	10.7	32.2	2,636	16.4	100
Engineering, technology	197	2.4	11.7	1,481	18.7	88.3	1,678	10.5	100
Agriculture, forestry and veterinary science	90	1.1	41.5	127	1.6	58.5	217	1.4	100
Biological and physical science	1,019	12.5	34.0	1,978	25.0	66.0	2,997	18.7	100
Administration, business, social studies	1,649	20.3	51.7	1,542	19.5	48.3	3,191	19.9	100
Architecture, other professional and vocational studies	82	1.0	37.3	138	1.7	62.7	220	1.4	100
Language, literature, area studies	1,528	18.8	76.8	462	5.8	23.2	1,990	12.4	100
Arts other than languages	747	9.2	52.8	667	8.4	47.2	1414	8.8	100
Multidisciplinary	825	10.2	56.4	638	8.1	43.6	1,463	9.1	100
TOTAL	8,125	100	50.6	7,924	100	49.4	16,049	100	100

Note: C = column, R = row.

Source: Data supplied by the Universities Statistical Record.

Table A10 Proportions of Welsh undergraduates to all UK undergraduates, and percentage differences from same-sex averages, 1991/92

Subject group	Welsh undergraduates as % of UK undergraduates			% difference of women from female average and men from male average		
	Women	Men	All	Women	Men	All
Education	4.1	4.6	4.2	−19.6	0	−12.5
Medicine and health	6.1	5.1	5.6	+19.6	+10.9	+16.7
Engineering and technology	4.0	4.6	4.5	−21.7	0	−6.3
Agriculture, forestry, veterinary science	4.1	5.9	5.0	−19.6	+28.3	+4.2
Biological and physical science	4.6	4.9	4.8	−9.8	+6.5	0
Administration, business and social science	4.6	4.3	4.4	−9.8	−6.5	−8.3
Architecture, other professional and vocational studies	5.5	5.3	5.4	+7.8	+15.2	+12.5
Language, literature and area studies	6.0	4.2	5.5	+17.6	−8.7	+14.6
Arts, not languages	5.4	5.1	5.3	+5.9	+10.9	+10.4
Multidisciplinary	4.4	3.9	4.1	−13.7	−15.2	−14.6
TOTAL	5.1	4.6	4.8	(5.1)	(4.6)	(4.8)

Source: Welsh Office (1993a) Table 8.09.

113

Table A11 Welsh postgraduates at university in the United Kingdom, by subject group and gender, 1992/93 (December)

Subject group	Female N	C(%)	R(%)	Male N	C(%)	R(%)	Total N	C(%)	R(%)
Education	435	35.4	58.2	312	19.9	41.8	747	26.7	100
Medicine and health	100	8.1	57.1	75	4.8	42.9	175	6.3	100
Engineering and technology	32	2.6	11.4	249	15.9	88.6	281	10.0	100
Agriculture, forestry, veterinary science	20	1.6	46.5	23	1.5	53.5	43	1.5	100
Biological and physical science	186	15.1	28.0	478	30.5	72.0	664	23.7	100
Administrative, social and business studies	265	21.5	52.0	245	15.6	48.0	510	18.2	100
Architecture, other professional and vocational studies	59	4.8	54.1	50	3.2	45.9	109	3.9	100
Language, literature, area studies	64	5.2	62.1	39	2.5	37.9	103	3.7	100
Arts other than languages	55	4.8	40.4	81	5.2	59.6	136	4.9	100
Multidisciplinary	14	1.1	45.2	17	1.1	54.8	31	1.1	100
TOTAL	1,230	100	43.9	1,569	100	56.1	2,799	100	100

Note: C = column, R = row.

Source: Data supplied by the Universities Statistical Record.

Table A12 Proportions of Welsh postgraduates to all UK postgraduates and percentage differences from same-sex averages, 1991/92

	Welsh postgraduates as % of UK postgraduates			% difference of women from female average and men from male average		
	Women	Men	All	Women	Men	All
Education	7.4	7.9	7.6	+32.1	+46.3	+38.2
Medicine and health	4.1	5.0	4.5	−26.8	−7.4	−18.2
Engineering and technology	4.1	5.8	5.5	−26.8	+7.4	0
Agriculture, forestry and veterinary science	5.6	4.4	4.9	0	−18.5	−10.9
Biological and physical science	5.6	5.4	5.5	0	0	0
Administration, business and social studies	4.4	3.8	4.1	−21.4	−29.6	−25.5
Architecture, other professional and vocational studies	6.7	6.3	6.5	+19.6	+16.7	+18.2
Language, literature, and area studies	7.2	5.0	6.1	+28.6	−7.4	+10.9
Arts other than languages	4.2	4.1	4.2	−25.0	−24.1	−23.6
Multidisciplinary	2.4	5.1	4.0	−57.1	−5.6	−27.3
TOTAL	5.6	5.4	5.5	(5.6)	(5.4)	(5.5)

Source: Welsh Office (1993a) Table 8.10.

Table A13 Open University undergraduate students in Wales, course registration, by faculty and gender, 1990 to 1992

Faculty	N	1990 F C(%) R(%)	1990 M C(%) R(%)	N	1991 F C(%) R(%)	1991 M C(%) R(%)	N	1992 F C(%) R(%)	1992 M C(%) R(%)
Arts	695	31.8 65.2	11.8 34.8	708	31.5 67.2	10.9 32.8	751	30.5 66.3	11.8 33.7
Social sciences	757	29.8 56.1	16.1 43.9	722	27.1 56.6	14.8 43.4	804	29.5 59.8	15.0 40.2
Education	127	6.3 70.9	1.8 29.1	149	7.4 75.2	1.7 24.8	138	6.3 73.9	1.7 26.1
Mathematics	620	8.8 20.2	24.1 79.8	664	9.2 20.9	24.7 79.1	660	8.9 22.1	23.9 77.9
Science	497	10.7 31.2	16.6 68.8	512	11.1 32.6	16.3 67.4	539	12.9 39.0	15.3 61.0
Technology	689	7.2 14.9	28.5 85.1	712	6.8 14.3	28.7 85.7	731	5.8 13.0	29.6 87.0
'U' courses	78	4.1 74.4	1.0 25.6	142	5.8 61.3	2.6 38.7	147	5.4 59.9	2.7 40.1
'K' courses	20	1.2 85.0	0.1 15.0	24	1.3 79.2	0.2 20.8	12	0.7 100	0 0
TOTAL	3,483	100 (40.9)	100 (59.1)	3,633	100 (41.6)	100 (58.4)	3,782	100 (43.2)	100 (56.8)

Notes: Teaching year runs from February to October; thus study year 1992 equating to the ordinary 1991/92 academic year.
'U' courses = cross-faculty interest and relevant to broad range of students.
'K' courses = small number of courses; may count towards Diploma in Health and Social Welfare.
C = column, R = row.

Source: Welsh Office (1993a) Table 9.01.

Table A14 Open University undergraduates by gender, age, and whether new/continuing, 1992

Age	Total	New F C(%) R(%)	New M C(%) R(%)	Total	Continuing F C(%) R(%)	Continuing M C(%) R(%)	Total	Total F C(% R(%)	Total M C(%) R(%)
Under 21	14	1.0 28.6	2.2 71.4	2	0.1 50.0	0.1 50.0	16	0.3 31.3	0.6 68.7
21–24	50	1.5 12.0	9.8 88.0	62	3.0 53.2	2.1 46.8	112	2.6 34.8	4.0 65.2
25–29	110	3.1 10.9	21.9 89.1	317	11.2 38.5	14.2 61.5	427	9.1 31.4	16.1 68.6
30–34	115	4.3 14.8	21.9 85.2	482	17.7 40.0	21.0 60.0	597	14.2 35.2	21.3 64.8
35–39	118	10.5 34.7	17.2 65.3	505	19.7 42.4	21.2 57.6	623	17.2 40.9	20.2 59.1
40–44	107	13.3 48.6	12.3 51.4	468	19.9 46.4	18.3 53.6	575	18.2 46.8	16.8 53.2
45–49	103	18.7 70.9	6.7 29.1	252	11.6 50.0	9.2 50.0	355	13.4 56.1	8.6 43.8
50–54	76	18.2 93.4	1.1 6.6	143	6.7 51.0	5.1 49.0	219	9.7 65.8	4.1 34.2
55–59	84	17.9 83.3	3.1 16.7	96	4.1 46.9	3.7 53.1	180	7.8 63.9	3.6 36.1
60–64	49	10.0 79.6	2.2 20.4	75	3.5 50.7	2.7 49.3	124	5.2 62.1	2.6 37.9
65 +	12	1.5 50.0	1.3 50.0	61	2.5 44.3	2.5 55.7	73	2.2 45.2	2.2 54.8
TOTAL	838	100 46.7	100 53.3	2,463	100 44.2	100 55.8	3,301	100 44.8	100 55.2

Note: C = column, R = row.

Source: Welsh Office (1993a) Table 9.04.

Table A15   Full-time teachers in non-university higher and further education, by gender and grade, 1990 and 1992

Grade	Total N	1990 F C(%) R(%)	M C(%) R(%)	Total N	1992[1] F C(%) R(%)	M C(%) R(%)
Principals	43	0.2 7.0	1.3 93.0	38	0.3 10.5	1.1 89.5
Vice-Principals	43	0.4 11.6	1.2 88.4	6	0.1 33.3	0.1 66.6
Other Heads of Departments	207	1.9 11.1	5.9 88.9	7	– –	0.2 100
Readers	3	0 0	0.1 100	3	0.1 66.6	(0) 33.3
Principal Lecturers	258	1.3 6.2	7.8 93.8	15	0.1 13.3	0.4 86.7
Senior Lecturers	1,272	18.7 17.9	33.5 82.1	1,394	23.3 22.5	36.3 77.5
Lecturers	2,505	77.4 37.7	50.1 62.3	2,867	76.1 35.9	61.7 64.1
TOTAL	4,331	100 28.1	100 71.9	4,330	100 31.2	100 68.8

Note: [1]1992 figures provisional
C = column, R = row

Source: Welsh Office (1993a) Table 7.05; and data supplied by the Welsh Office (provisional pending publication when supplied).

Table A16 **Full-time university staff, by grade and gender, University of Wales and GB, 1992 (31 December)**

Grade	University of Wales Total N	F C(%) R(%)	M C(%) R(%)	GB Total N	F C(%) R(%)	M C(%) R(%)
Professor	321	1.5 2.5	13.2 97.5	5,510	2.4 5.1	12.9 94.9
Reader/Senior Lecturer	585	5.9 5.5	23.4 94.5	10,359	9.8 11.0	22.8 89.0
Lecturer	1,691	69.8 22.5	55.4 77.5	30,412	67.1 25.7	55.9 74.3
Others	312	22.9 40.1	7.9 59.9	5,776	20.7 41.7	8.3 58.3
TOTAL	2,909	100 18.8	100 81.2	52,057	100 22.4	100 77.6

Note: C = column, R = row.

Source: Data supplied by the Universities Statistical Record.

Table A17 **Enrolments at LEA adult education centres, by mode of study and gender, 1991/92**

	Total N	Female C(%) R(%)	Male C(%) R(%)
Part-time day	20,312	30.7 80.1	20.5 19.9
Evening only	52,395	69.3 70.2	79.5 29.8
TOTAL	72,707	100 72.9	100 27.1

Note: C = column, R = row.

Source : Welsh Office (1993a) Table 10.02.

APPENDIX IV. LETTERS TO FE COLLEGES AND TECs REQUESTING INFORMATION FOR THE STATISTICAL SURVEY

Letter to FE Colleges

TR/JMC

11 January 1994

Dear Sir/Madam

Equal Opportunities Commission study of the position of women in education and training in Wales: request for information

We have been commissioned by the Equal Opportunities Commission to conduct a study into the current situation of women in education and training post-school in Wales. The scope is comprehensive as regards the type of education, training and organised learning, and embraces formal public settings of provision, private training, and various non-formal initiatives and programmes. The study will bring together the results of relevant research to provide the context and it will compile and review as much information as possible in the time allowed concerning initiatives and programmes to promote women's participation and gender equality in education and training.

The main part of the study is a statistical analysis of the situation using data from relevant sources to describe and analyse the position of women in education and training in Wales today. The data analysis will also review the sources and coverage of quantitative data on these issues. The end result, in addition to the analysis and the critique of existing data sources/coverage, will be recommendations for change emanating from these parts of the study. It is about data on the position of women, and gender distributions, in FE that we seek your co-operation.

Though some of these matters are covered in the 1993 Welsh Office statistical publication up to the year 1991/92, we should be extremely grateful if you could supply us with information on:

– gender distribution (numbers and, if possible, percentages) of enrolments and students on courses, by course and by full-time or part-time mode of attendance: current and 1992/93;

– gender distribution of course completions by type of course and mode of attendance: 1992/93;

– gender distribution of the destinations of full-time students (as well as other students or trainees if available) on completion or leaving: 1992/93.

Any additional breakdowns of the three main categories of data we are seeking in terms of age of student, ethnic origin, and first language will be most gratefully received.

The project officer mainly responsible for this statistical part of the study is David Istance, who is also a Senior Research Associate at the School of Social and Administrative Studies, University of Wales, Cardiff. Any queries about this request will be gladly answered by David at his University office (address: 62 Park Place, Cardiff: CF1 3AS; tel. (0222) 874000 ext. 5184; fax: 874436).

Please send your contributions to the work to David Istance directly or Teresa Rees here. We need them by the end of January so that they can be incorporated into our report in the course of February. Any other material you have that you think will be relevant to this, or any other aspect of the project, will also be most gratefully received.

We look forward to your cooperation in our study, and will be glad to send you a copy of the final report when it is published by the EOC.

Yours sincerely

Dr Teresa Rees
(Senior Research Fellow)

David Istance
(Consultant to the project and Senior Research Associate, University of Wales, Cardiff)

Letter to TECs

TR/JMC

19 January 1994

Dear Sir/Madam

Request for statistical information on gender in contribution to the on-going Equal Opportunities Commission (Wales) study on the position of women in education and training in Wales.

We have been commissioned by the Equal Opportunities Commission (Wales) to conduct a study into the current situation of women in education and training post-school in Wales. The scope is comprehensive as regards the type of education, training and organised learning, and embraces formal public settings of provision, private training, and various non-formal initiatives and programmes. The study will bring together the main results of relevant research to provide the context and it will compile and review as much information as possible in the time allowed concerning initiatives and programmes to promote women's participation and gender equality in education and training.

It is as regards the other main component of the work that we write to you. An important element of the study will be an analysis of the situation using statistics and data from as many relevant sources as possible in order to describe and analyse the current and evolving position of women in education and training in Wales today. The data analysis will also seek to review the sources and coverage of quantitative data on these issues. The end result, in addition to the analysis and the critique of existing data sources/coverage, will be our recommendations for change emanating from these parts of the study. It is about the position of women, and gender distributions, in data held by the TECs that we seek your co-operation.

Though some of these matters are covered in the 1993 Welsh Office statistical publication up to the year 1991/92 and other publications, we would like to extend and update those statistics. Therefore, we would like to know for your TEC area (and we are making the same approach to the others in Wales):

i) YOUTH TRAINING

i)a Gender distribution (numbers and, if possible, though not necessarily, percent ages) of starts in YT in your TEC area: most recent information and trends based on quarterly or the approximate monthly 'time period' returns going back as far as data permit;

i)b Gender breakdowns for the same time periods as i)a of the SOC groups of YT trainee starts;

i)c Gender distribution of completions in terms of job outcomes, NVQs, and any additional destination data as is available for the same time periods;

i)d Any further breakdowns that may be possible to calculate of i)a - c concerning age, ethnicity, disability, or other special needs categories, or else an indication that existing data do not permit gender patterns for these additional breakdowns to be calculated.

ii) ADULT TRAINING

ii)a - dSame breakdowns for ET as for the YT categories above. As regards ii)d any additional breakdowns might include information on employment/unemployment history, such as whether the trainee is a 'returner' and whether normal 6 month unemployment requirements have been waived because of domestic responsibilities.

iii) OTHER TEC PROGRAMMES WITH A SIGNIFICANT TRAINING COMPONENT

This request concerns any quantitative information about patterns and levels of enrolments; the equal opportunities officer in the TEC may well be subsequently otherwise approached by one of us concerning initiatives and programmes for women's employment and training. Here we specifically ask for any additional statistics the TEC might possess concerning patterns and trends regarding participation in specific programmes such as Women into Management and Business Start-up courses.

The project officer mainly responsible for this statistical part of the study is David Istance, who is also a Senior Research Associate at the School of Social and Administrative Studies, University of Wales, Cardiff. Any queries about this request will be gladly answered by David at his University office (address: 62 Park Place, Cardiff: CF1 3AS; tel. (0222) 874000 ext. 5184; fax: 874436).

Please send your contributions to the work in paper copy to David Istance directly or Teresa Rees here. We need them by the end of January so that they can be incorporated into our report in the course of February. Any other material you have that you think will be relevant to this, or any other aspect of the project, will also be most gratefully received.

We look forward to your co-operation in our study.

Yours sincerely

Dr Teresa Rees
(Senior Research Fellow)

David Istance
(Consultant to the project and Senior Research Associate, University of Wales, Cardiff)